THE SUDAN PEOPLE'S LIBERATION MOVEMENT/ ARMY (SLPM/A)

A Systematic Crisis for South Sudan 1983-2013

Rule from the top, the Liberators, Warlords, Political Cronies, Public Resource Scavengers who use power and corruption that breed an expensive selfish lifestyles and prestige of their Oyee Culture!

JULIA AKER DUANY & WAL DUANY

Bloomington, Indiana, USA

authorHOUSE®

AuthorHouse™
1663 Liberty Drive
Bloomington, IN 47403
www.authorhouse.com
Phone: 1 (800) 839-8640

Published by AuthorHouse 08/23/2018

ISBN: 978-1-5462-0780-1 (sc)
ISBN: 978-1-5462-0778-8 (hc)
ISBN: 978-1-5462-0779-5 (e)

Library of Congress Control Number: 2017913907

CONTENTS

PART ONE

     The North-South Problem

     Conceptions of Governance

     Centralization of Government of Sudan

     The rise of SPLM/SPLA

     Cultural Groups Involved in the Liberation Struggle

     Conflicts between the SPLM/A and Anya-Nya II Movement.

     The Ethnic Alignments

     The Assassination of the Any-Nya II leader Samuel Gai Tut

     Absorption of the Anya-Nya II Movement

Marxism and the Sudan People's Liberation
Movement/Army (SPLM/A)

Assault on Indigenous Institutions and Values

AK-47 the Military Power

Creating Differences within the Communities

System based on Security of the Few

Social Delinquency and Recklessness

Public Interest and Organization of Society

The process of disengagement from SPLM/A

Development of the Syndrome of Asymmetry

The SPLM/A Factions

The Sudan People's Liberation
Movement/Army (Mainstream)

Ideological Objective of SLPM/A (under John Garang)

The Sudan People's Liberation Movement/Army (United)

Organizing Principles of the SPLM/A-United

The Nuer Indigenous Defense System

Ngundeng's Social Concept of Nation

Mobilization of Military Capabilities

Method Organizing for Security and Defense

Limiting Shirking

Purpose of Mission: Peace Facilitation

Places and People Visited

PART TWO

ACKNOWLEDGEMENTS

THIS BOOK IS the culmination of many years effort, which involved many friends, colleagues, grassroots communities and many other stakeholders in South Sudan. Naturally, there are many to acknowledge, thank them for their support and appreciate them for their belief in this book, some of whom are featured in the book and some who were behind the scenes helping to make this book possible.

First, we express our deep and heartfelt thanks to the entire staff of my publishing team for generous support to finish this book to final publication.

This book is in the spirit of 2.4m people who had paid with their blood in the two civil wars of Nya-nya and the SPLM/A and those who will be paying the price of freedom after the independence in defending their liberties.

We acknowledge and thank all contributors to the book collective voices whish helped to shed light on what have become the most highly recognized liberation movement in Africa and the lost hope and the aspirations of the people of South Sudan under the leadership of the SPLM/A. The pride we carried during hey days of liberation in 80s to 90s and shame we endured after the independence.

For those who contributed substantially to this book in ways other than providing full account of incidents and stories, we deeply thank you as well. You provided perspectives, contacts and moral support for which we are grateful. We single out very wonderful two individuals Late Dr. Alfred and Audrey Heasty, the South Sudanese Friends International team, Jerry and Isabel Hogue, Jack and Sharon Schmidt, Prof. Erick Rasmussen and all the members of the Grace Presbyterian Church in Bloomington, Indiana, the Department of African Studies, Indiana University for their support from the very beginning of our mission to Sudan.

Our search for truth and peace took us to so many people in Africa, Europe and USA, starting with office of Congressman Johnson, World Council of Churches, Basel Mission and Reform Church of Germany, Presbyterian Church USA, All African Council of Churches and particularly, the Kenyan Government under the leadership of President Moi Kabaki and his predecessor President Daniel arap Moi for their commitment to see through that there must be peace in Sudan, we thank you very much indeed. We thank many South Sudanese Dinka and Nuer Chiefs who were very much committed to the welfare of their communities and hosted us so dearly at very difficult times. A special word of thanks is extended to Late Chief Malual Wun, the paramount chief of Western Nuer who serviced his people for 59 years and to Chief Gum Mading of Warrap State for their strong leadership; the members of the Presbyterian Church of Sudan, particularly the New Sudan Council of Churches under the leadership of Moderator Rev. Matthew Mathiang Deng and his team. The young people who gave inside stories, Makal Doul, Kiir Toung and so many others young South Sudanese whose dreams have dashed.

There are too many people to mention, however, we are grateful for all the help in moral and in-kind facilitation we got from wonderful people in many countries who care about this book and who shared their perspectives of the quest of South Sudanese for peace.

While each of you contributed in different ways, the most important thing you did for us was to make us feel welcome and know that we had grassroots communities as supporters behind us who believed in this undertaking mission. And many thanks to millions of South Sudanese who are enduring and watching the river of blood of their love ones had been pure down for them to be free and it is heart-breaking for them to see that they are being put in the same situation by their leaders who lost vision and are being driven by quest for material interests.

We thank our family and personal friends, especially Dr. William Lowery and Davis Adam who stood by us when we were constantly busy traveling and sometimes getting so many setbacks working on this publication. As the saying goes, "it takes many minds to build a nation", surely many minds had contributed to this book.

And lastly, my (Julia) tribute to my dear departed husband, late Hon. Prof. Wal Duany who dedicated his life to service his people and his memory is still alive and well with us. Even though he did not live to witness the December 15, 2013 incident where many of our people were mowed down on streets of Juba, Malakal, Bor and Bentiu. The time we spent working on this book was one of the greatest experiences in our lives searching for peace for our people. Now, the history is repeating itself, I am alone on the same mission again in 2013 trying to find out what had gone wrong again that our people had to be subjected to these nightmares by the same leaders is a very difficult task to bare and a long agony to overcome. I (Julia) never thought that one day our people will be running away from their own government, where, the selfish and savages' behavior of the leaders had rip apart our communities politically, economically and socially.

December 15, 2013 didn't come by a surprise to most South Sudanese who have over the years despondently watched things get out of Kiir's hands in an atmosphere of rampant corruption, resource mismanagement, nepotism and all their attendant socio-economic ills which reached alarming proportions. The masses have for far too long suffered from the adverse effects of the destructive acts of economic sabotage, ethnic patronage and various others irregular practices by a hand full of the so-called top SPLM/A members and officials in the office of the president.

Wherever you turn, our people are agonizing over undemocratic government hidden agenda and policies of dominance, repression, subjugation, terror, lack expression, lawlessness, insecurity, discrimination, favoritism, tribalism, nepotism, poverty, corruption that breed underdevelopment in South Sudan. Kiir's government had taken a bold crack-down at high speed on those who think that South Sudan need change to build better institutions to save the country from collapsing. The government policy over freedom of expression had taken toll on the citizens and outcry has been what Noam Chomsky stated, "If we don't believe in freedom of expression for people we despise, we don't believe in it at all." His policies are directed towards experienced journalists who lost their lives trying to inform public of the ill practices of Kiir's administration.

This book is to provide information and a call for genuine leadership that hears people's voices, puts peoples' welfare first, places institutional development in the center and creates a vision of the future founded on liberty, justice and economic sustainability to improve people's livelihood. Otherwise, it would be very shameful of our leaders not to acknowledge the millions of South Sudanese who have labored without recognition that it is their blood that liberated people of South Sudan. The future of country is at stake including all those who stood up for freedom and demanded accountability, responsibility and respect from those who have claimed to be our leaders. We may never know most of their names, but the freedom and dignity they struggled for many ordinary South Sudanese will never be forgotten but their names are known and they shall be written in any real South Sudanese heart.

Oh! God Bless South Sudan.

Julia Aker Duany

ABBREVIATIONS

ANC	African National Congress
AU	African Union
AUHIP	African Union High Level Implementation Panel
BEG	Bahr el Ghazal
CAN	Civil Administration of New Sudan
CCSS	Coordinating Council of Southern Sudan
CPA	Comprehensive Peace Agreement
DoP	Declaration of Principles
DUP	Democratic Unionist Party
EDF	Equatoria Defense Party
GNU	Government of National Unity
GoS	Government of Sudan
GoSS	Government of South Sudan
HAC	Humanitarian Affairs Commission
ICC	International Criminal Court
ICG	International Crisis Group
ICSS	Interim Constitution for Southern Sudan
IDP	Internally displaced person
IGAD	Inter-Governmental Authority on Development
IGADD	Inter-Government Authority on Drought and Development
IMF	International Monetary Fund
IPF	IGAD Partners' Forum
JEM	Justice and Equality Movement

JIU	Joint Integrated Units
KPA	Khartoum Peace Agreement
LRA	Lord Resistance Army
NCP	National Congress Party
NDA	National Democratic Alliance
NDI	National Democratic Institute
NEC	National Election Commission
NISS	National Intelligence and Security Service
NLC	National Liberation Council
NRM/A	National Resistance Movement/Army (Ugandan movement)
NSCC	New Sudan Council of Churches
OAG	Other armed groups
OAU	Organization of African Union
OLF	Oromo Liberation Front
OLS	Operation Lifeline Sudan
Paanluelwel	South Sudanese Bloggers
PCP	Popular Congress Party
POC	Protection of Civilians
PDF	Popular Defense Force
PNC	Popular National Congress
PPLF	Political Parties Leadership Forum
RCC	Revolutionary Command Council
RSS	Republic of South Sudan
SAF	Sudan Armed Forces
SANU	Sudan African National Union
SCP	Sudan Communist Party
SLM/A	Sudan Liberation Movement/Army
SPDF	Sudan People's Democratic Front
SPLM/A	Sudan People's Liberation Movement/Army
SPLM/A-FD	Sudan People's Liberation Movement/A –Former Detainees (Leaders)

SPLM/A-IO	Sudan People's Liberation Movement/Army in Opposition
SPLM-DC	SPLM-Democratic Change
SSDF	South Sudan Defense Force
SSFI	South Sudanese Friends International
SSIM	South Sudan Independence Movement
SSLA	South Sudan Legislative Assembly
SSLA	South Sudan Liberation Army
SSRB	South Sudan Referendum Bureau
SSRC	South Sudan Referendum Commission
SSRC	South Sudan Rehabilitation commission
SSTV	South Sudan Television
TMC	Transitional Military Council
TPLF	Tigris People's Liberation Front
UDF	United Democratic Front
UDP	United Democratic Party
UDSF	United Democratic Salvation Front
UP	Umma Party
UNMIS	United Nations Mission in Sudan
UNMISS	United Nation Mission in South Sudan
UPDF	Ugandan People's Defense Force
USAP	Union of Sudan African Parties
WUN	Western Upper Nile
WWW	Wine, Women and War

MAP

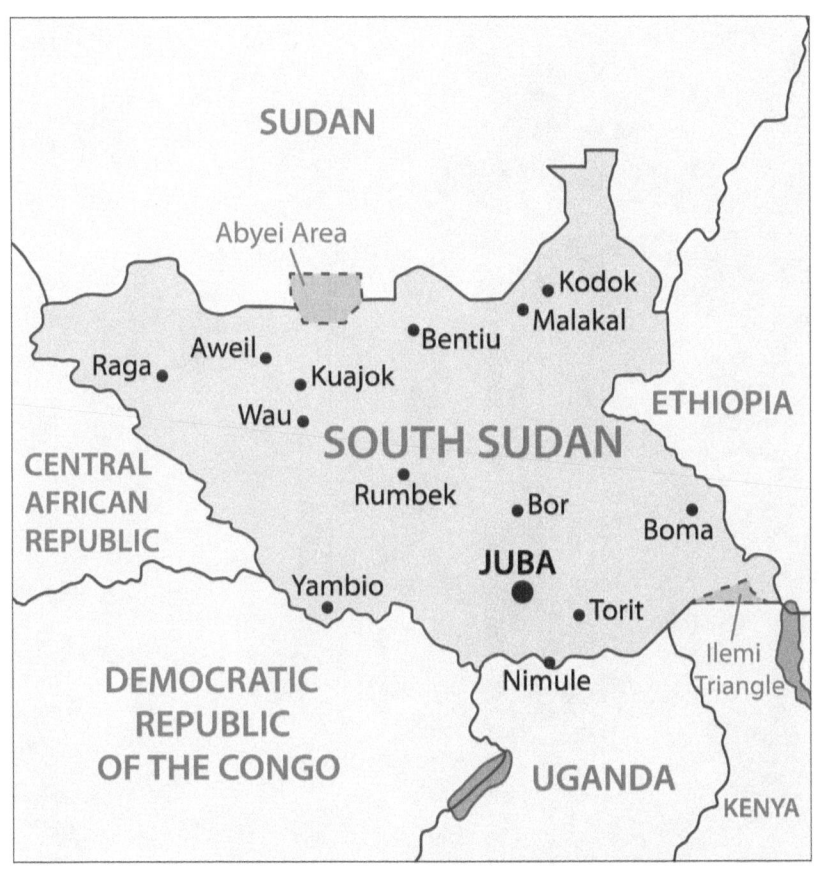

World Vision Hong Kong: Famine Declared In South Sudan:
2017, February 22

SHARE FEELINGS

Dedicated to all Victims of December 15, 2013 Massacred

We were bitter but we forgave

We cried and laugh at times

We were sad but we smiled

We were worried but we gained confident

We remembered and we forget

We hope for time when our people will cry no more

We hope for that time, we hope for the time

We shall not forget because we know your names

Your names are written in our hearts

They are truly written in our hearts

(Julia Aker Duany, January 2016)

PREFACE

Africa is a continent of surprises, nothing is ever quite
as it seems and nothing happens quite as it is supposed
to (David Lamb)

THE STORY OF struggle South Sudanese has been told in many
different versions sometimes tragic and sometimes giving hopes.
Many scholars has been giving messages no less necessary and elevating
than it was to the South Sudanese of the 19th century. The story is to
presents timeless of noble people moving towards catastrophe, dragged
down by their leaders selfishness in accumulation of wealth and power,
cursed with immorality and murdering of the their own citizens, this was
the legacy of those SPLM/A members who lead Comprehensive Peace
Agreement (CPA).

We want to remind the readers that we too in the 21st century need to be
told that man is but a limited and had been contingent creature, subject
to sudden disrupting forces. Many stories of told about the success of
the South Sudanese struggles, however the success is not finally to be
measured by fame or material wealth achieve by SPLA/M. Human
greatness consists ultimately in nobly accepting the responsibility of
being what we are; human freedom, in the personal working out of our
fate in terms appropriate to ourselves. Though we may be innocent,
we are all potentially guilty, because of the germs of self-sufficiency;
selfishness and arrogance are in our nature. We must remember that
always that we are only human-beings and modest in our own conceits.
Our place in the total pattern of the cosmos is only finite. That is not to

say that it may not be glorious. Whatever our circumstances, we achieve and endure through to essential greatness. It is not what fate has in store for us that matters, but what we do with it when it comes. No power, no imposition, no catastrophe, can uproot the personal dignity of each human being. The seeming caprice and unfairness of life, striking some down and pampering others, is only the beginning of the Great Encounter, both the choice and the destiny are ours. (Paul Roche 1996).

I (Julia) also read a book written by the Winner of the Noble Peace Prize, Professor Wangari Maathai, and tittle *"The Challenges for Africa"*; disappointed by African leaders, she wrote that *"I was on the wrong bus."* The book focuses on the African leaders and how they manipulate the people to stay in leadership as long as they are life and kept dragging the lives of Africans in poverty. I agreed with her whole heartily; many Africans find themselves supporting bad governments just because is headed by their tribesman. As we still keep hoping, a few Africans leaders have worked in their countries to find ways for ordinary people to find justice, peace, respect and dignity; finds route out of poverty, ignorance, lack of healthcare, education, violations of basic rights, corruption and so many other problems associated with Africa. It is our hope that South Sudanese immolate those few African leaders, like President Mandela and others who champion the course of freedom for their people.

We, (Wal & Julia) did still hold hope that the work we have done through our grassroots peace-building, helping our communities so that they can improve their livelihood through share understanding and self-reliance. It is these experiences at our academic work, at the grassroots level; couple with our services in the Sudan and Southern Sudan governments and participation in numerous international efforts and research works to assist our people to find sustainable peace that have shaped our worldview and inform the approaches, analysis, examples and stories that we offer in this book.

As we work harder, it seems that things were getting worst. The evils genius were working to frustrate the good work done by many caring people in South Sudan and to illustrate more on this is driving home painful truth and this is what we have just done. SPLM/A after the war of liberation have achieve very little of what it stand for but this system/rule became a curse which South Sudan will have to take many years to cleans itself. As admitted by Garang himself that in the early 1980s, "SPLM/A is a mop of individuals organized to fight Khartoum Arabs led government. Khartoum government is too deformed to be reform, its only needs strong men to fight it". He was not interested in putting together a professional arm forces or a system that will provide guidance to the new nation. Now South Sudan is struggling to contain this mop of individuals, with few citizens who are trying to prevent the nation going bankrupt sooner or later and above all, they have to come to reality that the SPLM/A system had become a failure and they will have to look for alternative system.

This book is looking back of what has become of the largest African Liberation Movement, the Sudan People's Liberation Movement/Army (SPLM/A). Since its establishment in 1983 many of our people believe and put their full support behind the movement as the only way out of miseries of the united Sudan under the Islamic Arabs domination. Down the road of the 30 years of struggle many of our people were left in the trenches to pursue their own interests and ambitions; others have become disappointed, tired and died. Some are languishing in their homes disabled or jails; increase of the number of orphans and widows/widowers, others are homeless or in refugee camps and UNMISS sites seeking protection. Others are having high hope for leadership to deliver them; others are waiting until it is clear to them that they must save themselves, in the words of Mahatma Gandhi, being "the change they wish to see in the world".

Since 2005 under the leadership of Kiir and his policy of "Zero tolerance to corruption", South Sudan was hit with the bizarre set of immorality and corruption cases which have exposed SLPM/A party members, ministers and army commanders – and even the media headlines are full of the leadership names being call – as either corrupt, gang of looters, or stupid leaders. The most notorious of these cases involve the three ministers of finance – known as Dura Saga where the country's resources were looted by brief-case businessmen working in partnership with government officials and members of parliament. The case that made headlines news was the 60 million dollars between Pagan Amum, the secretary General vs former minister finance Author Akuen which died a natural death in the judiciary. Another empathic situation was the list of shame; naming the top SPLM/A leadership members including the members of parliament. This was the letter of 75 names sent out by the President asking his Ministers, commanders and party leadership members to return the 4 billion dollars that was taken in the treasury; whereas the records of the Government of Sudan revealed the real amount was over 20 billion dollars that was received by the Government of South Sudan from 2005-2013 (International Crisis 2013). And the leadership of August House who had taken loans from the Nile Commercial Bank and never repay the money which led to bank bankrupt.

Since 2006, the Newspapers caries Headline News of corruption stories by the ruling party members. For South Sudan to survive in this environment of high corrupt practices need a tremendous labour for the citizens to yell the words "Judgment for all the corrupt officials!" It is a phrase that resonates with the populace but given the daft ears by the leadership. Lack of services has been catastrophic for the SPLM/A led government. The corruption that has been going on in the party and government was holding nation resources to ransom by just a handful of people, the SPLM/A political gangs, commanders and their immoral allies. For example the people of South Sudan had been asking whether the presidency is in the center of corruption. The citizens are wandering why they are giving a blind eye to this grave embezzlement of public resources. These cases were very clear, the 288 million dollars for Awiel road was given to the President own company, the Ayaat Company; the Telecommunications Services companies, GemTel and the Vivacell that generate tax-free millions of dollars were not known who own these companies? The presidential advisor used 7 million dollars to purchase a piece of land in Juba town; there was a Presidential break in and stolen millions of dollars and the officials who were implicated got away with it, the Ministry of Roads and Bridges with the construction of the Juba International Airport that took over ten years and never finishes with millions of dollars pumped into the project; Ministry of Land and Housing with electricity and water project which never brought electricity and water to Juba city; Ministry of Water Resources with Water Cooperation have never improve the urban and rural water systems; education and health systems are in shamble with the millions of dollars pumped into these sectors; Crisis Management Committee know as CMC; a body created to response to the December 15, 2013 crisis ended-up misappropriating the funds. The well-known phases in Juba town were, "it is our time to eat". This body was led by the Vice President; Hon James Wani Igga, the Minister of Finance and Economic Planning, Hon Aggery Tissa Sabuni and the Minister of Cabinet Affairs, Dr. Martin Elia Lomoro became another rout of resources mismanagement in South Sudan. Instead of visiting affected areas the members went to places that were not affected by war using all the resources and never account for it. The most disgraceful institution is the organized forces which in disarray, commanders squandering soldiers' salaries and all others well known corrupt cases that just dies in the air. The list just never ends and no one knows who is doing what? For Kiir leadership the right hand does not know what the left hand is doing. All these cases are well known to the ordinary people on the streets in all the towns of South Sudan. It has been over ten years and no one has been held accountable and the whole culture of corruption had become a pride for those who are known as big-men of the SLPM/A party and people wonder if there will be ever any accountability to get back these public resources (Gordon 2015, Christopher 2015).

The SPLM/A system was set by Dr. Garang a genius who had been flattering public with his smart speeches which fell in deaf hears of the SPLM/A members. One of his most popular quotes proves what is happening today in South Sudan: "The SPLM/A is a forum in which citizens shall have right to ask their government representatives where are the hospital and the school buildings and the roads you promise to construct? The SPLM is a forum in which citizens have right to report a member of the SPLA to face justice in the court of law if he/she has committed a crime against civilians". These are still questions being asked in 2017 by the public and they wonder why the SPLM/A had done so little to avert this grave situation. And why the President Kiir turns a blind eye to all these, is it for fear of his men turning against him. If this situation is not salvaged what will be the guarantee that SPLM/A government will save the South politically and economically. One of the SPLM/A members who is an MP one time put it in a simple Dinka term (*Bany aci thor cok*) the chief got speared in the foot by his own clan men. The meaning of this statement is that the chief is not innocent but he is the leader of the whole operation. The President is the Commander-in-Chief of the arm forces, but how can he does not know that his poor soldier goes for 4-10 months without pay. These soldiers have families who need food on the table. Where will the poor Soldier go?

The SPLM/A system make sure the security is kept tied and whoever criticizes the leadership is seen as an enemy of the people. This kind of system can tells us that the people who run it are canny and understood basic facts of oppressing others in order to enable them to loot the public resources to breed their expensive lifestyle. The leaders make sure that their children are send to best schools in Kenya, Uganda and other western countries so that they should have better opportunity. The accumulated wealth enables the rich man to marry multiple wives and many concubines as sign of social status. This created inequality among the SPLM/A commanders and the start of the failure of the institutions and the political system that were setup by movement which contributed to instability of economic system in the country.

The poor management of the government benefited one ethnic group, few political cronies and those who sang the songs of the big man. This had opened the door of moral deprivation; something has gone wrong with liberators. The norms of the society had changed in way that so many have lost their moral compass, and this says something significant about our today society. The liberators have forgotten the whole cause of why we lost over 2 million people in the war of liberation. They had forgotten that the Arabs system of governance of injustice and abuse of citizens creates resentment and protest that are all motived by unfair political and economic mismanagement which was manifested in the last fifty years of Sudan rule.

The December 15, 2013 crisis that created mass graves in Juba, Bor and Malakal answered so many questions which were asked by the public since the establishment of the SPLM/A in 1983. Are these Liberators or gang of looters coming together to kill and loot the country? This is where we borrowed the concept of being on the *"Wrong Bus Syndrome" that our people (South Sudanese) are on the wrong bus of SPLM /A* that have no destination. The South Sudanese, particularly the Nuer and other ethnic groups are all traumatized by physical displacement and confined to consternation camps in UNMISS/POC camps. They are not alone in pain; there is anger and frustration in the whole country, but our leaders do not see that our communities are deeply divided.

The commander class, only serve those who desire the status-quo. The support for the Big-man system creates a political culture that simply encourages autocrats and dictators. The system of commanders' class creates also one party system where leaders do not tolerate differences. These leaders think that they have been mandated to do whatever they please, killing, looting and behave unethically as if the world is their own, they really have lost their *humanness*.

Yet as we seek to indicate, the challenges before South Sudan not only regional or international influences, but are also a moral, spiritual, cultural and even psychological in nature. The 38 years of struggles had a big impact on our people, as one time said by the Hilde Johnson, the head of UNMISS that, "South Sudanese are rudest people in the world." May be the war we fought had created the culture of bad-manners but Miss Johnson knows she was a good friend of the SPLA/M and that we all share one humanity; there is no escaping from reality of what happened on December 15, 2013. We also thanks Miss Johnson for her great leadership, if she did not open the gates of UMISS to the seventy thousands Nuers, the world would have seen another Rwanda. These people are alive today because she did not allow Kiir's mow down and kill the Nuers in the pretexts of 1991 Bor incident. The reality is that Kiir had admitted that he plan the Juba massacre as a respond to the 1991 Bor killings, which he said, "Riek killed a lot of Dinka and we will not give him the opportunity to do so again." Although, the Bor incident was not plan by Riek, however, Kiir from many of his speeches as in the past always brought out his character as a simple-minded SPLA commander who toiled the liberation journey without understanding the doctrines from the more enlightened Drs. John Garang, Riek Machar, Lam Akol and Mr. Joseph Oduho (Juba Monitor, 2015).

The president kept the light of unti-Nuer burning even after ten years of 1991 Bor incident, he still reminded South Sudanese that there is a need for Nuer to pay the price and they should pay dearly. In fact before 1991, there were 1985, 1987, 1988 and many other incidents where many incent Nuer people were killed and this is not an issue to Kiir (Amnesty International 1988). The December 15, 2013 and July 2016 massacres were by design the State. The catastrophe became real for many South Sudanese citizens. The regime arrogant, stubbornness and look of no concern for the deteriorating social, economic and political crisis seem to be paying off for Kiir to stay long in power (Nyaba 2014).

We wrote *The Sudan People's Liberation Movement/Army: Institutional Crisis 1983-2013* for all those with an interest in the fate of the South Sudanese, from the general reader to advocates, researchers, development specialists, political parties, civil society's organizations and behind the grumble over leadership, the challenges facing the South Sudanese and importantly, to encourage all our people to stand-up for their rights.

SPLM/A Institutional Crisis Institutional Crisis is divided into two parts: the brief historical background, North-South Conflict and cultural groups of the South Sudanese, conflict between Anya Nya II and the SPLM/A movements, SPLM/A and Civil Population, the emergence of an alternative liberation movements, the peace mission and its accomplishments, and the purpose and what was done (chapter 1-7); part-two covers SPLM/A from the period of 2005-2013, the covenant and society in South Sudan; reflecting on the challenges facing the South Sudan as a new nation and we argue South Sudanese to support each other in their efforts to forge their own way forward and to believe that they can get away from someone agenda that has been set to destroy their dream of prosperity (chapter 8-9).

As I (Julia) finish writing this book, the South Sudanese have long experienced the fallout of such greed and selfishness, watching our leaders engaging a rat-race and savaging on the state resources in stiff competition that who will out-do the other person and emerge as the champion on the top of all thieves. It is a sad game being watched by the poor citizens of South Sudan. The crisis of December 15, 2013 offers South Sudan a useful lesson and its greatest challenges; they understand that nobody knows all the solutions to every problem; rather than God's intervention, South Sudanese need to pray hard, think, act and learn from their grave mistakes. One of the MP stated that, "The majority of South Sudanese are standing by the road side while the SPLM/A members are strangling the country. They are not liberators but just warlords and cronies with no country in their hearts." Another person called on the Miraya Radio and said that, "we are tired of SPLM/A, because when they get together they loot us, and when they fight they killed us."

All stories of mismanagement of the public resources was put together by a young South Sudanese Artist David Garang in which he related in one of his song the suffering of the ordinary SPLA soldiers on the streets of Juba. The song goes, "it is not right for our soldiers to go naked, bare footed and begging on the streets, it is not right. Where is the New

Sudan, the country they fought for?" Edmond Yakana, one the civil society leader stated that, "to save the name of the liberation it is time to put SPLM/A in the national museum for historical records and that their time has come to climax. The tools for liberation are different from the tools of building a new nation".

PART ONE

WHAT HAS BECOME OF SPLM/A
1983 - 2011

CHAPTER ONE

Introduction

THE LAST THIRTY-ONE years have witnessed a serious crisis of unity among the South Sudanese within the Sudan People's Liberation Movement and the Sudan People's Liberation Army (SPLM/A). In the 1983, 1991 and 2013 crisis all are manifested in the social and communal cleavages by which the SPLM/A political and social order are threatened. SPLM/A has not been able to address this crisis. SPLM/A's institutional order, how it works and defines the problem and its possible solutions, are themselves substantial sources of the tensions and all the conflicts in South Sudan.

In many cases, these actions of contentious social forces that challenge uniform views within the movement are perceived as disloyalty, betrayal of the movement, or an attempt to undermine leadership, unity, and stability of the movement. Instead of exploring ways of accommodating those forces through conflict resolution and covenantal arrangement, leaders have insisted on ruthless measures such as torture, imprisonment, or killing. The patterns of response to problematical situations, has generated an organization where the Commander in-Chief of SPLA exercises absolute and unlimited authority. Since 1983, this structure of dominance has yielded temptations that have encouraged some SPLM/A leaders to use the coercive power of their position to oppress, exploit, and wage war upon other South Sudanese.

Shocking, but the truth is use of displacement innocent people as part of the game of war as a method by which the commanders accumulate wealth to benefit from people's displacement is a strategy. The SPLM/A leaders campaigning in their names is a byproduct of feeing soldiers and providing them with cover, protecting their families made-up of multiple wives is the ultimate goal prolong the war itself. The leaderships make sure that they are taking the country on the joyride as long as their families are being saved and secure in the foreign countries.

The personalization of authority, predation, and repression has led to disengagement as a means of survival for individuals and communities in South Sudan. The process of disengagement is evident in the emergence of an alternative liberation movement. The SPLM/A-Mainstream, of course, opposed this alternative arrangement and did everything it could to eliminate it. Inter-group fighting resulted from the splits and the hard hand of the SPLM/A leadership to the squalled the rebellions leave no understanding but create more conflicts. The conflict escalated into destructive violence. With request from our community who were much concern on the situation on the ground, we (Julia and Wal) accepted their call and decided to attempt to mediate between the leader of the SPLM/A Mainstream, Commander John Garang, and the leader of SPLM/A - United (the breakaway group), Commander Rick Machar.

The following is a description of our mission to the South Sudan and an analysis of our observations of 1983 - Present. We will first describe the problem in the Sudan. Second, we will consider the crisis of unity in between the Anya-Nya - II Movement and SPLM/A. Third, we consider the relationships between the SPLM/A and the South Sudanese civil society. Fourth, we describe the emergence of the SPLM/A-United and later known as South Sudan Independence Movement/Army (SSIM/A) as alternative liberation organization and its consequences. Fifth, we explored the conflict between the rival liberation organizations and between northern and Southern Sudan. Lastly, I (Julia) considered where we are now, since 2005 to 2013, compare to the 1983-1990s. While Wal was sick and in his death-bed, on December 20, 2012, he asked me to whether there is anything good in Juba politics, we both laughed and I replied there is nothing new in Juba; it is the same old stories of male chauvinist, ignorance, corruption, and the three (WWWs) womanizing, wine and war. The integrity and morality among the SPLM/A leaderships has become a challenge to many South Sudanese citizens. In 2009, I remembered one time in a conversation; the former Chief Justice, Mr. Ambrose Ring Thiik is now a leader of Ginka Elders who asked Dr. Wal Duany, 'who really gossip with the President'. Wal replied, 'I thought you do?' They both laughed, because no one knew what was going on in the presidency.

According to Dhol Acuil Deng (1987) and also observed by John Young, 2013, although the majority of northern Sudanese leaders derive some of their legitimacy from religion, in practice the leaders of the liberation movements are ultimately not that different. Young wrote, the functions of the typical means liberation movements organize themselves in which one person holds both the senior military and political positions. This is designed to ensure there are no divisions at the top and that the political and military approaches are in sync, but it creates a context that encourages the centralization of the power and breeds dictatorship. The SPLM/A under Garang is a case in point. Indeed, as Salva Kiir graphically put it in one of the SPLM/A meeting 2004, "Garang carried the SPLM/A around with him in his brief case." Although Kiir has shown himself to be more conciliatory, the fact remains that he also holds enormous powers and currently carry the government as his own brief case (John Young 2007; Thot 2012). Kiir-led SPLM/A had resisted democratic transformation and South Sudan has failed to reach the definition of statehood because it has sustained, perpetuated incompetent and corrupt system of governance.

Is there anything new or just the same old story of SPLM/A? The rhetoric of the ideology of the New Sudan had died and replaced by the constructed immorality, abuses and insults, intimidation and violence on the citizens that they were not liberators, they did not experience the bush life, they did not carried the AK47, 'South was not liberated by pen but by AK–47.' The meaning of the whole program in South Sudan is that the SPLM/A members should be allowed to loot the country's resources by will. The party members' gang-up to plunder the nation, it became the politic of peer-groupings, greed and terror. The hotel nights in Juba, Kampala and Nairobi for different types of the SPLM/A groups, good food, drinks; albeit, even champagne bottles, cognac, black and green-level Johnny Walkers whisky and beautiful women walking between executive suites glamorize the hotels lobbies. While the poor South Sudanese are lingering in the displacement camps under sever sun, wet rains and diseases taking their lives in numbers that will never be recognized in the time of peace. But only remain in the hearts of their love ones.

The SPLM/A leadership has been out of touch with the people of South Sudan, and the people have suffered greatly in the hand of ruling party, the system is brutal and leaders have been involved in criminal activities, they are driven by evils and the vices of an immoral society. Since the independent of South Sudan in 2011, SPLM/A ultimately transformed itself into extractive institution under the control of a narrow elite and commander class that monopolized both political power and economic opportunities. The absolutism persisted through two years after the independent and the reform efforts were frustrated by the usual fear of creative destruction and the anxiety among the ruling commanders and elite group within the SPLM/A that they would lose economically and politically. The intense tribal warfare and destruction of communities led to total collapsed of the social structures among the South Sudanese society.

CHAPTER TWO

Background And History

The North-South Problem

HOW TO ACHIEVE peace in the Sudan was a problem of long standing since 1955-1972. The second Civil War between northern and southern Sudan broke out as early as 1975, but destructive violence escalated gradually. It has intensified since 1983-2005 and again in 2013 and 2016. The absence of consensus between northern and southern Sudan on the constitutional system of ordering political, economic, and social relationships has adversely affected the stability of the country, the absence of agreement on a system of governance has been compounded by the commitment of Government of Sudan to Islam and to the primacy of the Arabic language. Because this book is concerned only about the second civil war, we will consider the Aanyanya II movement and the Sudan People's Liberation Movement as the key actors along with the Government of Sudan with inclusion of the current South conflict after the independence 2011.

CONCEPTIONS OF GOVERNANCE

Ideas organize the thinking of individuals and the way in which human beings perceive their environment. Systems of ideas containing conceptions of the nature of the World in conjunction with value systems, affect the ways in which individuals treat one another and shape institutions structures.

How people think about themselves, their relationships with each other, and their relationships with the larger World are essential elements in what constitutes a people and their way of life. These common understanding are based partly on similar experiences in the past and partly on basic conceptions of universal order. Individuals think of and justify their own constitution of order in terms of their conception of their place in a universal order.

Conceptualizations of political order vary among the different culture groups living in the Sudan. Some communities such as the Anuak and Shilluk are organized as federated kingdoms (Duany 1993:2). Many also have the tradition of autocratic arrangements, especially, in the northern Sudan. Still others are known as acephalous societies. These are societies without a common head. Mary Douglas noted that these acephalous societies lacked both palaces and prisons and that regulative ideas or law emerged from social interactions (Douglas, 1980: 61-62). These traditions are held to be important in ordering these different communities, and they should be taken into serious account in constituting a new political order for Sudan as a whole.

The choices people make in selecting organizing principles are, therefore, not uniform, although many scholars have tended to believe that there is only one, hierarchical way to order human societies. This view ignores the way in which diverse cultures, operating in different local environments, have realized significant potential in the past. Submission to the basic constitutional commitment of the Government of Sudan and Government of Southern Sudan to pursue a monolithic (Arab Islamic) society implies the extinction of the diverse cultures and different ways of life in the South Sudan and in other parts of Sudan such as the Nuba and southern Blue Nile. Instead, members of the National Islamic front, the ruling party in the Sudan and the one which holds the most extreme views, believe that they have access to absolute truth, and that they should rid the Sudan of those who insist on divergent truths of their own.3 Their thinking is simple, Islam and Arabic language hold a key to united Sudan.

CENTRALIZATION OF GOVERNMENT OF SUDAN

Nimeiri's coup of 25 May 1969 instituted a secular, socialist state, with regional administrative autonomy for the South in recognition of the fact that the Islamic state favored by the main northern parties (Umma Party, Democratic Union Party [DUP], National Islamic Front [NIF] would be detrimental to national unity. Nimeiri, however actually began negotiations with the Southern Sudan Liberation Movement (SSLM) after he lost his communist supporters in 1971. The negotiations resulted in the signing of the Addis Ababa Agreement that ended 17 years of civil war in 1972. The agreement also led to the formation of a southern regional government, the first attempt to give a "Voice" to the Southern Sudanese in their own country since independence in 1956.

Despite reference to Southern autonomy, the structure of Nimeiri's regime was grounded in a conception of dominance. Its monopoly of prerogatives of governance closely resembles that of the previous governments of Sudan in the south. Dominating, Islamizing and Arabizing the Christians South were objectives shared by all the dominant political groups in the north before and after Nineiri's coup. They were clearly expressed by the most prominent leaders of the sectarian parties in the north. In January 1962, for example, the Minister of Education Sayed Ziada Arabi, asserted in a speech at Juba that national unity implied the universal adoption of Arabic as the national language and Islam as the national religion (Sanderson and Sanderson, 1981).

In his maiden address to the constituent assembly in October 1964, Sayed Saddiq el Mahdi, the Prime Minister, said: "The dominant feature of our nation is an Islamic one and its over powering expression is Arab, and this nation will not have its entity identified and its prestige and pride preserved except under an Islamic revival" (Mahdi,1966). Dr. Hassan El Truabi, the leader of the Islamic Front, expressed himself in a similar vein. He argued that the people in the southern Sudan had no unified culture, so this vacuum would necessarily be filled by Arab culture in the course of an Islamic revival.

In the process of implementing these policies, attempts have been made by the Government of Sudan to create an Islamic national identity. Arabic was introduced as the administrative and educational language, although English remained the medium of instruction in all Sudanese Secondary schools since 1967. Friday replaced Sunday as the weekly day of rest in the Christian south, Islamic conversion is encouraged, but Christians are not allowed to proselytize Moslems. Apostasy by Moslems under the 1991 Criminal Act is punishable by death.

Nimeiri's centralized government did not permit southern citizens to exercise the powers and responsibilities promised in the Addis Ababa Agreement (Alier 1991, Garang 1993, Duany 1987). Thus, the treatment of the southern Sudanese in civil and military matters was still dictated by Khartoum; the nature of that treatment made southerners second class citizens in their own country. Some southern military officers rebelled in Akobo in 1975 led by Gen. Gordon Koang; others rebelled in Wau and Juba in 1976 in which high top officers were killed, Gen. Abur Matuong, Gen. Jibiril Makol Mangong and other young officers. These military personnel fled across the Ethiopian border and established what become known as the Aanya-Nya II Movement. This group began hit-and run guerilla warfare against the Government of the Sudan in the Southern Region.

The Anua-Nya II later attracted additional members of the Southern Armed forces who deserted because of the deterioration of the political situation in the country. The division of the southern Sudan into smaller regions was the catalyst for the southern rebellion. Gen. Joseph Lagu, former Vice-President of the Sudan and President of High Executive council in the South, the proponent of the division of the southern Sudan in to small regions thought the division would alleviate the majoritarian domination of the major ethic groups, especially, the Dinka. 4. Lagu did not see any reason to fear the northern Sudan because that region was also regionalized. He assumed incorrectly that regionalization meant the federalization of political relationships in the nation.

The replacement of the single south region by three smaller ones was decreed by Nimeiri without applying the principles of amendment embodied in Nimeiri's own national constitution. Amendment of the Addis Ababa agreement required a three-fourths majority vote in the National Assembly, confirmed by a two-thirds majority vote in a referendum in the South. Division of the South made it clear to many southern Sudanese that better future depended upon a different political arrangement with the North, not participation in the regional (administrative) government. Some Southerners joined the Anya-Nya II Movement while others, including John Garang, established the Sudan People's Liberation Movement and its military wing, the Sudan People's Liberation Army, in 1983.

Garang death and after signing of the CPA agreement, the interim and independent ears 2005 to 2014 were challenging times for South Sudan. The Comprehensive Peace Agreement (CPA) signed in 2005 turned out to be a shady affair, rushed by those in a hurry to birth an independent South and welcome by the South Sudanese people with jubilation; to them the independence was a start of the new journey. But many critics like Professor Mahmood Mamdani saw that the people of South Sudan are just beginning to pay the price for that haste. CPA was not well thought-out by the international community; they gave full support to empower SPLM/A and the NCP parties creating two states under their dictatorship.

Mandani (2014) also wrote that the CPA was premised on a militarist assumption that only those with the capacity to wage war have the right to determine the terms of the peace. The talks, thus, rendered illegitimate the political opposition in both the north and the south at the stroke of a pen. Doubling as both army and movement, the Sudan People's Liberation Amy/Movement (SPLM/A) in the south emerged as the precious double of the National Congress Party (NCP) in the north. The story had not changed, in case of the country, patriotism apart, the SPLM/A in all its forms had dragged the nation to a fail state. They confidentially have no regard for the lives of the South Sudanese. Their illustration, the rest are simply collateral damage. The SPLM/A leadership, consider the people are part of the bigger scheme in a game of wild hunting. The politics SPLM/A during the war was coupling with chairman controlling system. This was also carried on that the leader of government during the relative peace must not change and will never change as long as the SPLM/A is in power (Opoka 2015).

Following the referendum, South Sudan became autonomous in 2005 and independent in 2011. The CPA reinforced the most negative of the legacies of the liberation war. The sense that 'liberators' could do no wrong reinforced the aversion to internal reform and laid the seeds of the present crisis of December 15, 2013 in which over 20,000 Nuer people were massacred by the government forces in Juba, leave alone the other towns such as Bentiu, Bor and Malakal were many lives were lost in what the SPLM/A in Opposition called the revenge killings.

The majority of people South Sudan have been thinking that they are free, however, this sad chapter of our liberation brought in the reality which we been so long in denial. Opaka 2015, describe it as follow, "just because we drive cars, buy expensive food, drink late in the night, sleep with foreign women, travel abroad, own homes, bank accounts in foreign banks and send money aboard to our astray wives and still walked heads up". The citizens have been just reduced to zombies waking up in the night to slave for their masters only to return to their graves at day light. The elites, elders and the real brave sons and daughters of South Sudan who love this country had gone into hiding because of fear of their lives, letting the scavengers slay incents, loot and accumulating power and material resources to satisfied their selfish needs (Juba Monitor 2015).

Not did this young man (Opaka) took upon himself to save his nation by picking the pen to confront the evils but he had awaken other South Sudanese to see where the country is going. He stated that, "if you are a general in the army and see your country going to ruins and remain silent, you are much complicit in the destruction of your country as the very people destroying the nation".

We agreed with this statement and it is the very reason we did pick-up the pen to write because we have over seven hundred members of parliament in national and state houses that are thieves, selfish, cowards and ignorance about their job. They do not stand up for the truth and only truth shall make this nation be free. A young man called on the Miraya Radio to sharing his feelings about the MPs and stated, "The two houses of legislators of our country are meeting places for the thieves to set strategies how to loot the nation. They are ally partners in destruction of our country".

CHAPTER THREE

The South-South Conflict

The rise of SPLM/SPLA

THE RISE OF SPLM/A is grounded on the failure of the government of Sudan to implement the Addis Ababa Agreement. The Addis Ababa Agreement was made to promote autonomy and economic well-being of the peoples of the Southern Sudan. Both of these goals failed to be achieved.

The underlying problem of the Addis Ababa Agreement was basically that it was done in bad faith by Nimeiri. As already mentioned earlier in this book, in 1971, Nimeriri negotiated the Addis Ababa Accord with the Southern Sudan Liberation Movement (SSLM); only when his support from the Communist Party declined and the Islamic ideology fill in the political vacuum. This meant that he did not care for a solution to the problem of the Sudan but to get support that would keep him in power. Nimeiri was highly supported in the south after signing this Addis Ababa Agreement that support later declined as soon as he tempered with Addis Ababa Accord in 1982.

When he reconciled with Umma Party and NIF and a number of prominent members of Umma Party and National Islamic Front (NIF), Nimeiri thought he did not need the support of southern Sudanese. He took certain actions to ensure the destruction of the Addis Ababa

Agreement. First, Nimeiri's government attempted to change the border lines between western district of Upper Nile region (where there are petroleum deposits of commercial quantity) and the southern District of southern Kordofan of the northern Sudan. The government also tried to change the border line between Renk District of northern Upper Nile the southern Sudan (where most of the Sudan grain production is carried out) and the Blue Nile Province. These attempts were frustrated by southern Sudanese. Change of border demarcation of the South, according to Addis Ababa Agreement, required three fourths votes in national parliament and two-thirds vote in a referendum in the South.

The second action by Nimeiri was an attempt to transfer to the northern Sudan the Anya-Nya military units based in the South in accordance with the Addis Ababa Agreement. This attempt was again seen by Southern Sudanese as a violation of Addis Agreement. The command ordering the Anya-Nya soldiers to go north was rejected by the troops in those units in the South. This mutiny started the destructive civil war in Bor town of Jonglei Province; this was beginning of the second civil war in 1983.

The introduction of the September Laws of 1983 (Islamic Law) was the third provocation of the South to rebellion. These laws made the Sudan an Islamic Republic and Christians were reduced to second class citizens. In addition to September Laws, Nimeiri with the support and agitation of Muslim colleagues from the Umma Party and the National Islamic Front (NIF), decreed into law the division of the southern Sudan into three smaller regions. The imposition of the division of the South into its original three smaller regions was the catalyst of the rebellion.

Cultural Groups Involved in the Liberation Struggle

The early involvement of cultural groups in the liberation struggle was caution and limited. This caution and the limited entry into the movement were in the first place due to lack of information about the strategies and goals of the movement. Second, the people of Equatorial believed that the SPLM/A was a response to the recent division of the South into three smaller regions. Since Equatoria supported the division of the South, which was initiated by the North, the people of the Equatoria Region saw very little in the movement for them and did not join it until later after the fall-out of John Garang and Riek Machar. People of the Nuba Mountain people also were late in involving themselves with the liberation struggle. The Nilotic groups, Nuer, Dinka, Shilluk, Anuak were the early peoples involved in the liberation struggle.

The Nuer are a people in southern Sudan; most of the land is located in the hydrologic region known as the Southern Clay Plain of the Nile River Basin. The Nuer way of life is largely pastoral. The Sudd region (flood lands) of the White Nile is the principal source of water during the dry season. People move their livestock on a regular cycle to pools, lakes, lagoon, marshes, and river channels in the dry seasons and to higher pastures during the wet season.

The Nuer people are often identified as a paradigm case of an acephalous society-a society without a head or central authority. The Nuer as an acephalous society has a close kinship to federal societies, if the term "federal" is construed as pertaining to a "covenantal society." The Nuer have a strong covenantal tradition but without the "formal" political apparatus that is commonly associate with two or more "levels" of government in a federal system of government. These are, however, import features of Nuer society pertaining to ideas of covenant, breach of covenant, and reestablishing the bonds of covenantal relationships that have important implication for all covenanting societies.

The Dinka are Nilotic people in the Southern Sudan. The majority of Dinka are/is located in west of Nile, Barh el Gazal region, but some Dinka communities of various sizes live in Upper Nile region and others the Abeyi Dinka live in Kordofan region in the northern Sudan. The Dinka like the Nuer are an acephalous society. However, within some Dinka segments, there are more "centralizing" instruments of government than among the Nuer.

Certain Dinka clans have hereditary ritual and supply the priests, who symbol of office is the sacred fishing spear known as 'Beny Bith'. Among the priestly clan, a single "master of the fishing spear" is acknowledged as pre-eminent. Those who do not belong to the priestly clans are warriors and like the priestly clans acknowledge a single leader. The authority of the spiritual and secular leaders is slightly the same. The warriors or the secular leaders freely change their allegiance from one spear master to another (Collins, 1971: 55-56; Godfrey, 1956).

The other Nilotic are made-up of Lou groups, Acholi, Annuak, Shilluk and Jur. The Shilluk are a Nilotic speaking people living on the west bank of the Nile north and south of Fashoda in the southern Sudan. Shilluk cultivate the land and keep only a few cattle. The Shilluk are a Kingdom and are well known of their centralized system of governance. The Kingdom is divided into districts, each with its own head, all of which recognize, the Reth or "divine king" of the Shilluk.

The Anuak, like the Nuer, Dinka and Shilluk are a Nilotic speaking people. They live east of the Nuer at the foot of the Ethiopian escarpment. The Anuak like the Shilluk, maintain a <u>Nyiye</u> or "divine king."

The Bantu or Sudanic linguistic groups are Ndogo, Balanda, Bongo, Kreish, Baka, Madi, Moru are found both in western Bahr el Ghazal and western Equatoria. The Eastern Nilotic groups are found in eastern Equatoria region and they are Toposa, Boya Lotuka, and Didinga. The Bari speaking groups are the Bari, Mundari, Pojulu, Kuku, Kakwa and Mudu in central Equatoria.

The Nuba are the Bantu (Negroid) Africans located in the Nuba Mountains in the South-eastern part of Kordofan State in the northern Sudan (Nadel, 1947:1-15). There is a sizable number of Christians in this predominantly Muslim region. Nuba are a confederation of different speech communities and the Nuba are Agriculturalists and keep few livestock.

Conflicts between the SPLM/A and Anya-Nya II Movement.

The ideology of the SPLM/A, which was Marxist, was detestable to the Anya-Nya II Movement. The SPLM/A ideology generated a structure of governance that does not take into account concepts of equality, freedom of action and deliberation to resolve conflict. Use of authority by the SPLM/A leadership was arbitrary. It was not bound by any knowable rules of law or ethical standards. It rendered judgment with a bullet. The Nuer and other smaller groups opposed this arbitrary behavior.

The Nuer presumption of the equality of all before their Creator gives individuals equal standing in transaction public affairs and it a right that is highly protected. Shared beliefs about what actions are consistent with respectful relationships among disparate persons are reflected in social rules. Some patterns of behavior are considered improper in certain settings and are not permitted. Other ways of behavior are perceived as proper and are therefore allowable or required. Temptations always exist for some to ignore these mutual expectations in pursuit of personal gain of some sort. When these rules could no longer be maintained, the advantages that accrued from these mutually respectful relationships gave way to hostility and breakdown of shared understanding.

The problem of the objective of the movement and quarrel over leadership compounded the problem of a communist ideology. The first bloody split unfolded in early stages of the founding of the SPLM/A (1983-85). The real issue was the direction of the struggle: one side called for an independent South Sudan, a call at heart of the Anya-Nya struggle and continued by the second struggle of Anya-Nya II under the leadership of Gai Tut, the other side called for a New Sudan under the leadership John Garang. The lack of agreement on what the war was all about, the leadership contest between Gai Tut and John Garang, and the communist ideology of SPLM/A could not be resolved by the leaders. Gai Tut, Akot Atem, Abdallah Chuol Deang could not agree with the SPLAM/A and later continued with the leadership of the Anya-Nya II Movement. John Garang became the sole leader of the SPLM/A. Garang declared war on the Anya-Nya II Movement with disastrous consequences. As recalled by Lual Deng in his book 2013 that Dr. John use to say during his various discourses with his associates, "My Southern Sudanese separatists would have to come with me first to Khartoum in order for them to achieve their goal of independent South Sudan".

This call on the elimination of separatists marks the first face of SPLM/A internal struggle. In 1984 Samuel Gai Tut, the leader of Anya-nya II was killed, William Abdulla Chuol succeeds him. Chuol is reported to be receiving support from the Government of Sudan and became a challenge to the SPLM/A forces of 105 Battalion under the command of Major John Kulang who defeated the Anya-nya II and its two commanders Abdulla Chuol and Akot Atem were killed; John Kulang got promoted as a reward, becoming the alternate member of the Political Military Command of the SPLM/A.

Years later Commander William Nyuon ordered the arrest and detention of Commander John Kulang. Kulang and follow detainees, including Comander Karubino Kuanyin Bol, Commander Arok Thon and many others were accused of staging a coup against Dr. John Garang. As they receive unjust treatment in detention center and out of bitterness, Kulang took all these treatment as unjust incarceration, escaped from the detention center and joined the Sudan Government to fight the SPLM/A. He was later ambushed and killed by Commander Kerubino Kuanyin forces on his way to his home town Fangak. The method of demonizing and pitting each commander against the other had hunted many commanders in the SPLM/A. Commanders, William Nyuon, Kerubino Kuanyin and later George Athor also met their death in similar situation at the hands of gunmen who believed to have been either in the SPLM/A or once members. The death of these great men of South Sudan need deep research to present accurate history not a distorted one as we have seen in recent publications on South Sudan. To educate the generations to come we need to provide an objective historical accounts of this country call South Sudan with all ample analysis to shed light on actions of actors. The kind of narrative that is needed should justify and accommodates the good and the bad of their noble and the evil acts. Every actor has to be given their accurate contributions in the liberation of this great nation.

The Ethnic Alignments

South Sudan is a multi-ethic society. No ethnic group constitutes a majority, but the Dinka and Nuer make 58% of the population in the country. The Anya-Nya II Movement initially drew most of its support from the Nuer, while the SPLM/A drew most of its fighting men from Garang's people, the Dinka Bor. According to the late Joseph Oduho, 'the war within the war' in Southern Sudan was effectively a war between the Nuer and the Dinka Bor (Oduho, 1992). The Dinka having upper-hand and control of the movement gave them the power to wage a horrible war on the Nuer villages. The Gaajak, Gaajok, Lou and Gaaguang Nuer were subject to the torch. Women, children, and elderly people were massacred. Many were maimed by the use of anti-personal mines (Oduho 1992; Wantok et al 1992.)

As this war went on some Nuer were recruited by SPLM/A as were Dinka of Barh el Ghazal and other peoples from the south and the Nuba region. But according to Commander Riek Machar, the war between the Anya-Nya II Movement and SPLM/A was a war fought effectively between two groups of the Nuer (those with Garang and those in the Anya-Nya II themselves.6

The warfare between the SPLM/A and the Anya-Nya II Movement was much more than a simple struggle for definition of the objective to be achieved. The objective could have been worked out as it was on it the

Washington Declaration. Neither was it a simple struggle for power. It was a struggle for a monopoly of control over the whole population. What was at stake, were not differences of opinions, as expressed by Gai Tut of the Anya-Nya II Movement (or latter on by the leadership of the SPLM/A –United), but the legitimacy of differing opinions. Garang's political maneuvering at the time and at the time of his death can only be explained as an effort to win absolute power for the socialists under his personal leadership. As long as both the Anya-Nya II Movement and SPLM/A exist, the southern people could choose between them and find support for their grievances. Success in eliminating his competitors or aspirants to leadership would have opened the road to the total control of resources and subjection of the SPLM/A as a single organization and the population of the southern Sudan to total socialist control and some invisible supporters, and also mean the control of resouces.7

The Assassination of the Any-Nya II leader Samuel Gai Tut

In 1982, one of the Anya-Nya war veterans, Gen. Samuel Gai Tut was not happy with Joseph Logu government policies of dividing the south into three regions. He decided to join his colleagues the leaders of the Akobo munity, Gen. Vincent Kuany Latjor and Gen. Gordon Kong Baypiny who already rebelled against the Nimari regime in 1975. They were later joined by Lt. Col. William Nyuon Beny, Major Kerubino Kuanyin Bol and Dr. John Garang de Mabior in 1983. As mention in the above section, what lead to disagreement between John Garang and Samuel Gai was a bout leadership, who should lead the movement, Samuel Gai wanted Akuot Atem to take the political leadership and Samuel himself to lead the command of the military and John Garang would take the chief of general staff of the army. This look like a fair shot but it did not go well with John Garang who wanted both political leadership and the control of the army. This was not accepted by Samuel Gai and his team and the reconciliation became a history. Garang was favored by the Ethiopian government of Mangistu Helimariem and whose interest was to team-up with Garang to advocate for a communist state in a united Sudan. Mangistu who had already benefited from the support of the Soviet Union bloc wanted to assert his influence on the hope to keep out the Western bloc lead by American and the its European allies from Sudan.

For two years, SPLM/A could not make a head way to do operations in South Sudan because the area was controlled by Anya-Nya II. Garang and Mangistu had to find way to get rid of Gai Tut group. In 1984, General Thokwath Pal, an Ethiopian Nuer was commissioned by the Ethiopian Government to bring the groups together for reconciliation. The plan was that the meeting location was to be in Adura, the invitation was then sent to Gai and his group to report to Adura for a reconciliation meeting. The objective of the meeting was to unite the forces so that they can be able to fight the enemy together on one front.

As Gai's group became suspicious why they were not consulted during the preparation and just to be told were the meeting was. As a military man he was always security minded, he then decided to assemble his group in a place call Bil Kuey some miles away from Adura, to wait for a massage from General Thokwath Pal. To their surprise they were attacked by military helicopter gunship in the air while the ground forces were command by John Garang group, under Kerubino Kuanyin Bol. This was a well-planned attack; it was very difficult battle for Gai Tut team to overcome the attack and they lost the battle. Samuel Gai group received major casualties; he was the first to be killed so was Akuot Atem and many others. The man who killed Gai was later identified as Chuol Tot, a man who was on the Ethiopian helicopter gunship to identify Gai Tut and the one who fired the shot that killed Samuel Gai Tut.

John Garang claimed the victory and declared that he is at war with the separatists who are his first enemies and his first bullet directed at them. Samuel Gai, a true son South Sudan whose blood was spilled by his own people. This was later admitted Nyang Chol in one his speeches during the December 15, 2013 incident that, "he was among those who killed Samuel Gai Tut and that he is also ready to kill Riek Machar as well" (SSTV 2014).

John Garang quest for leadership had a bad memory to many South Sudanese, particularly the Nuers, he never forgive his enemies. One of the young men who witnessed the killing of Samuel Gai Tut related the story that he will never forget what he had seen when he was eight years old. After Gai was killed he was buried in Adura. Some days later John Garang and the SPLM/A soldiers came to prove whether Samuel Gai did really died.

This young man related the story as followed, "when John Garang and the group of his body guards arrived the whole village was rounded-up at the gun point and they asked the people to show them the place where Gai Tut was buried. One elderly man showed them the grave, the soldiers immediately starting digging the grave to retrieve the body of Samuel Gai Tut. After they identified the body, Kairbino Kuanyin Bol ordered the soldiers to lash the dead body with 250 lashed in font of all the village people. This was to serve as a warning to others and particularly to the Nuer who were separatists. Human beings have lost their moral values, the sadness that begot Adura that morning and the Nuers who had seen one of their own being treated with humiliation was a moral degradation to them. Those who witnessed this undignified treatment are still bitter up today.

In his book, "Inside an African Revolution," on page 260, Dr. Lam Akol referring to an armed confrontation in the early stages of the movement points out that, "Samuel Gai Tut himself was killed during the fighting. This was March 30, 1984. His body and that of Akuot Atem were not discovered until two days later. On receiving the news, Dr. Garang and Kerubino Kuanyin Bol flew by a helicopter to Adura village where Kerubino lashed the decomposing body of Gai Tut fifty strokes while Garang looked on in appreciation. The body by then was beyond recognition were it not for the characteristic finger of Gai Tut."

Many questions were asked: why was the body of Gai Tut (a Nuer) mutilated and that of his fellow Dinka colleague was not treated the same. This sends a very disturbing situation to the Nuer community who saw their own being humiliated.

Anya-Nya II recollected its forces and waged war on the SPLM/A under the command of General Abdullah Chol; for three good years 1984-87 it was a nightmare for John Garang forces. They could not make a head way until the death of Abdullah Chol in 1987.

Absorption of the Anya-Nya II Movement

Although reconciliation and unity between the Anya-Nya II Movement and the SPLM/A was achieved in 1988 under the leadership of Daniel Kout Matthew, institutional arrangements were not put in place to guarantee broad participation in the decision-making process. The Anya-Nya II Movement was simply absorbed into SPLM/A structure. Contestation and argumentation were not institutionalized as mechanisms for conflict resolution. Attempts at contestation were made, but they were thwarted by the SPLM/A leadership. In May 1985, John Garang had dissolved the National Executive Committee (NEC) along with the entire Secretariat and other organs of the movement, and silenced all contrary views (Oduho, 1993; Aleu, 1992; Wanok, 1992).8

The SPLM/A leadership could not, however, command the effective participation of experienced and enlightened persons. Attempts to persuade the leadership to convene the National Congress in order to write the constitution of the movement, organized and carry out elections of its leadership were all in vain (Oduho, 1993, Aleu, 1992; Wantok et all).9 The only way a multi-cultural movement such as SPLM/A could be governed administered purely by a single ethnic group or a section thereof, the Dinka Bor, was by use of political terror. This was the course upon which the SPLM/A under Garang and socialist colleagues embarked.10

The rule of terror led to the establishment of an irresponsible liberation movement and massive destruction of peoples and property. The absence of institutionalized means of conflict resolution foreclosed the possibility of rationality formulating programs of action because, if alternative opinions cannot be expressed for the fear of punishment, torture, or death, decisions are made by one man in an absolutely arbitrary way. It complicated the problem of the legitimate succession of leaders, because, if no group of leaders could freely express their views, personnel policies had to be determined on the grounds of private connections, intrigue, and manipulation. By forbidding differences of opinion, the SPLM/A hastened its own degeneration and deadline in the capability of the people to cope with the daily challenges of life.

Garang used of isolation as a management tactic to guarantee loyalty to him. He makes sure you are isolated and even your friends fear to associate with you because the intelligence is all around you. The persons on isolation are not told their mistakes. Garang makes sure that they are cut off from assignments because these were all officers who collect their resources from the local communities, to rent homes and feed their large families, pay school fees and other needs. When the isolation weighs heavily on the victims, they succumb and go back to Garang to beg for mercy and forgiveness, even when they do not believe they are guilty. Garang use of terror to humiliate opponents and he use isolation and withdrawing of financial support from the families as part of punishment. This method of isolation resulted into many victims, eminent South Sudanese leaders became victims, Kuol Amuom, Hon. Dhol Acuil, Ater Dak, and many others. The only General who survived the isolation was Awet Akot because his wife befriend Garang's wife so that Awet could get his job back.

Marxism and the Sudan People's Liberation Movement/Army (SPLM/A)

The division of the Southern Region into three smaller regions led to exodus of many prominent South Sudanese from the armed forces and government ministries. These included Benjamin Bol Akok, Martin Mager Gai, Dhol Acil, Dr. Justin Yac Arop, Salva Kiir, Daniel Awet, Arok Thon Amok, Amon Wantok, Mager Aciek and many others. Some of these men believed that the South should remain one region in disregard to the wish of the majority.11 However, there were non-Dinka among the founders of SPLM/A. Some of these person included William Nyuon Bany, Joseph Oduho, Riek Machar, Elija Hontop, Lam Akol, Peter Adwok Nyaba and many others.

The underlying problem today in SPLM/A is that there were two groups. One group that initially articulates was that of Socialists. These persons were unionist in their Manifesto. The separatists was the other group within the SPLM/A. However, the separatists were supportive of the program of the communists group. The Socialists were supported by Mengistu of Ethiopia.12 The Marxists wanted to liberate the Sudan from a minority clique of "oppressors" (of Arab descent) who have dominated governance in the Sudan since independence in 1956. This was a concern to the majority of South Sudanese and they believed that this was a very narrow way of looking at the problem of the Sudan.

A redemptive potential arises from a competitive dynamic that increasingly concentrates power in a declining portion of the population constituting the oppressors, and a lack of power in an increasing portion of the population constitution the oppressed group. This is the source of the SPLM/A revolutionary potential that can be expected to yield the collapse of the existing bourgeois social order and the emergence of a new social system for the whole Sudan. Ironically the destruction of the "oppressors" is exceeded by the oppression, torture, and killing by those who proclaimed the liberation of southern Sudan as their goal. Description of this situation is given in the following section.

The North supports the unity of the Sudan provided they are able to stamp out the "separatist tendencies" of the people in the South (New Sudan 1986: 20-21). These separatist tendencies are currently represented by the SPLM/A-United led by Riek Machar who wants a referendum in the South to allow the people to make choices as to how they want to relate to the North. What save South was that Riek didn't get stripped up confusing the means with goals itself. He saw what was the need independent south and then chart a course for the future of South Sudan.

There was a problem of understanding of the intention of SPLM/A. The Democratic Unionist Party (DUP), one of the northern parties maintains that "generally our militia policy aims at creating a security belt against aggression from the forces of atheism and Christian colonialism under the leadership of John Garang the deserter, who does not bother to conceal his hatred of Arabism and Islam" (New Sudan 1986:20-21). This was a misreading of SPLM/A leadership. SPLM/A believes that Christianity, race, or common history do not provide the basis for unity of the southern Sudanese (Garang, 1993). It was Marxism under the guidance of Garang and his socialist group that can provide the basis of unity for the southern communities. Joseph Oduho maintains that "another source of anger against Garang stemmed out of the people discovery that Garang was not running a movement that was preparing its members to assume the administration of an independent southern Sudan (Oduho, 1992:-5-7). The SPLM/A regime, under Garang, was and still is an organization without institutional constraints long after Garang is gone and, therefore had and still has very limited potentials to learn from its mistakes.

It is by doing that people learn the art of governance. Without practice people are denied or have limited opportunities to learn. The "Soviet" type institutional order of SPLM/A was introduced as the ultimate means of solving Sudan's problems. Its leaders legitimized their power by claiming infallibility, that is, they could not acknowledge that they might make mistakes. Where there is error, there is no need for correction.13 The claim of infallibility makes it impossible, or at least difficult, for citizens to discover errors, all important proceedings are covered with a veil of secrecy. Until the Nasir Declaration of August 28, 1991, SPLM/A rule was a conspiracy of silence.14 Coercion and corruption have been the means of running the Sudan People's Liberation Movement. Coercion has not worked well because it ignores the need for the cooperation of ordering peoples.15

Corruption, as a technique for ruling over a society, is a negative strategy aimed at demoralizing and disarming a potential internal enemy, or at winning over and ally by compromising his moral integrity.16 Used widely, it demoralizes society. The corruptor cannot escape corruption him/herself. A positive strategy, aimed at providing the movement some political support and legitimacy, is reform. A reform strategy presents better possibilities for participation, but these concerns mostly the intelligentsia; ordinary people are entirely involved in the struggle for material survival as either displaced persons or refugees.

The root of Marxism-Leninism started in 1983 when a number of SPLM/A comrades were sent to one of the most prestigious school for revolutionary studies in Cuba. The focus of their studies was to study Marxism-Leninism and several others theories that would make them political commissars that will undertake and turn a simple SPLM/A solider to a tenacious revolutionary of Viet Cong fervidity. To be able to do this, they were told that the spirit of Marxism-Leninism requires them to elevate one person who will be a comrade Chairman or Secretary General and transform him/her into a supper-person possessing supernatural characteristics akin to those of a god. This person supposedly should know everything, sees everything, thinks for everyone, can do anything including firing or ordering fire squad of any subject without complain at all.

According to Aleu Ayyiny, such believe was cultivated into those members for one full year and then they were allowed to go back to the fields sent Sudan to spread the gospel as progressive officers. Their work was to make sure that they became the masters of developing the personality cult of the Chairman and all the members of the High Command and to make sure their security and survival is assured. This created a whole series of exceedingly serious and grave perversions of SPLM/A principles and the revolutionary legality. All members of High Command competed to be praised more in revolutionary songs composed by the soldiers and ordinary people. This was the beginning of the practical consequences resulting from the cult of these individuals and the accumulation of immense limitless power in their hands. Great harm was caused by the violation of the principle of collective direction of the movement which resulted into several attempts to depose the chairman by his fellow members of the High command and culminated into murder or lengthy imprisonment of several of most progressive officers. Other communist cultures began to developed such disinformation, fabrication, people being charged of being the enemy of people so many South Sudanese lost their lives, people like Benjamin Bol Akok, Lakurnyang and so many others.

CHAPTER FOUR

SPLM/A and the South Sudan's Communities

THE 21 YEARS of civil war had resulted into destruction of social structure of the South Sudanese society. It would be unfair to overlook the role play by the movement in destroying South Sudanese values and their peaceful co-existence; it was very clear since its inception in 1983. The SPLM/A adapted strategies of the Uganda National Resistance Movement, led Yoweri Museveni, this system has a very devastating concept, ruling by fear, making up lies and terror without allowing any room to accommodate different views that would question any act deem to the leadership as good. Therefore, for the movement to achieve what it want to do; certain techniques were used to polish its dictatorial and Marxist ideology and sometime it would goes as far as Hitler approach in shunning out the unwanted (race) or group of particular section of people and individuals. Here the ethnicity became the mark of cleansing the unwanted section of the society (John 1994).

The SPLM/A movement from the very beginning started creating ethnic clashes within the communities, favoring one community over other, siding and empowering one community in fighting against the other. Since then the war of destruction among the south Sudanese communities started and had never stop up to this dates until it broke out again in December 15, 2013 when the Kiir administration adapted the same divide and rule strategy.

The SPLM/A had been dominated by few individuals who used all the facilities to advance their quest for power and better living on the expenses of the majority of South Sudanese. To justified their cause they term others as traitors and disloyal. Whenever there is any disagreement questioning their ideology, or how things are being manage in the movement, that will be crossing of the line and it can amount to terror and punishable by death. Hon. Martin Majier Gai, a lawyer who wrote the SPLM/A first Manifesto was the first victim to be jailed right after the launching of the SPLM/A manifesto. That act was followed by the arrest and the killing of many others, whose fates are not known and yet to be determine in the whole story of the 21 years of South Sudan's struggle.

The most important problem that is entangled in the institutional crisis of the SPLM/A has to do with nature of the relationship between the SPLM/A and the civil population of the South Sudan. The way people think of themselves, their relationships with one another, and their organization are the important ingredients in what constitute a civil society. The structure of the institutions of the SPLM and the SPLA did not take into account the ingredients of life of the South Sudanese. The incompatibility was obvious to the Nuer who rebelled against the way the SPLM/A was treating them (Oduho, 1992; Aleu, 1992; Wantok et al,1992). This section of our book will describe the ways in which the nature of south Sudanese society contrasts with a communist-style institutional order and will explore the different effects of the interplay between the civil society and the SPLM/A.

There are four strategies that SPLM/A used to silence and subdue the public, (a) the power of the gun and terror, (b) creating differences among communities, (c) delinquency and recklessness, (d) disregard the communities values. The communities are treated as objects that do not have rights and have to surrender to the mercy of the military might.

Assault on Indigenous Institutions and Values

The early perception that the SPLM/A could be an instrument of the liberation of the south Sudan from northern Sudanese domination as led to attempts to strengthen its functional capacities. Unfortunately, far from liberating South Sudan, these efforts have largely led to the centralization and personalization of authority, corruption, greater predation, repression, and a declining of civic capacity to resolve local problems. The order of the day is left to the mercy of those who carry AK-47.

Establishing a "Socialist System" in all of Sudan was the main goal of the movement. The SPLM/A and its Manifesto were associated with efforts to achieve the salvation of all people in the Sudan, to liberate the oppressed, eradicate their oppressors to transform Sudanese society from a "bourgeoisified society" into a "new" (Socialist) society, hence the concept of the New Sudan was born. The gospel of Marx and Engels, articulated in The Communist Manifesto, explicitly repudiated all "religion," morality," "eternal truths," and presumed to act "in contradiction to all past historical experience "([1848] 1967:103), but was as "devoted to salvation as any Abrahamic prophet" (V. Ostrom, 1992:13).

The Manifesto (1983:21-22) of the SPLM/A divided the world into two camps: the "friends" and the "enemies" of the SPLM/A. Similarly, Sudanese Society was divided into a class system described in the philosophy of "scientific socialism." This system included the Socialists, revolutionary intellectuals, peasants, bourgeois, and petty bourgeois. The existence of these imaginary classes was propagated in the refugee camps in Ethiopia, within the units of fighting men in the southern Sudan, in the training places in Cuba, and wherever southern Sudanese were trained in socialist countries.17

People were taught that they had enemies within the close proximity. The impact of the teachings of some their communist ideas were greater among the types of people who are easily swayed from their traditional beliefs. The term "bourgeoisie", for example, caught the attention and imagination of semi-literate and illiterate part of the South Sudan Society (Aleu,1992:7).

Within the ranks of SPLM/A, some intellectuals claimed they were the Socialists. The Socialists were to be the beneficiaries as well as the custodians of the SPLM/A revolution. These individuals went about identifying people to stamp as bourgeois so that they could be isolated and destroyed (Aleu, 1992:7). The majority of intellectuals, former government ministers, representatives in the parliament, college and high school student, former military and police officers were all branded as reactionaries. They were considered as the "enemies within the movement" (Oduho, 1992, Aleu, 1992, Machar, 1993).18

The class system used by Marxists is not relevant among the Nilotic people of South Sudan, particularly, the Nuer and other southern peoples. Distinct groups that exit such as cattle rich, young and old, age-set and its disaggregation among the Nuer are perceived in a different light than the rigid classes of the early industrial period in the West from which Marx derived his conception of classes. The classes are used for the purposes of governance but sectors in an acephalous organization are use as linkage of communication. The elder lead authority is respected by the young as well as the young are to learn from the elders.

However, the Socialist or "Progressive officers" in SPLM/A used literacy and illiteracy to classify South Sudanese. The "literate" in the movement were those who held positions in the government by virtue of their education, which as former official of the Government of Sudan and high school and university students. The "illiterate" in the movement were those who could not read or write. The literates" were said to look down upon the "illiterates" viewed the literates with suspicions. This created mistrust and hatred among the civil population and was highly observed and re-en-enforced among the SPLM/A members.

The individuals, who were semi-illiterate and illiterate, were led by the propaganda of the "progressive officers" to view the educated in general, especially former politicians, with suspicion, and worse, with enmity and disrespect.19 Elders or educated, were called bourgeois by the young and uneducated. Parents and elders were called "comrades" by their children and relatives in defiance of indigenous respectful way referring to such people in society. Wives called their husbands "comrades". People began to wonder what that situation would lead to. This can be construed as a deliberate policy to destroy the way of life of the different communities in the southern Sudan. Dhol Acuil Aleu observed that the movement had "strayed into an unsurvey province" (Aleu, 1992). Why was this policy of destroying the values and tradition of society adopted? The explanation for this policy can be found in the Socialist belief that Socialism comes to power through agitation and conflict in societies. The mass persecution of intellectuals and educated people – anyone whose party loyalty might be doubted; led to terror and a huge waste of the society and resources. The leaders could get away with bad policies and enrich themselves at the expenses of the rest or because they thought it was good policies, a way of keeping themselves in power by buying the support of crucial groups of elites or powerful military men.

AK-47 the Military Power

The leadership of the movement believes that the only way to settle problems is through AK-47 the military might. They used of force and terror against anyone having grievances against SPLM/A member. In 1985-88, the SPLM/A waged wars against the Gajaak, Gajok, Gawaar and Lou Nuer that lasted three years, most of Nuer villages were destroyed and many lives lost, people were killed in a board day light with impunity. Until the death of Garang, nobody was brought to books and these destructions had not been a part of the SPLM/A story. The Anya-Nya II was view by many communities in South, particularly in Upper Nile as an alternative movement because they soldiers were living among the communities without fear. This was a threat and SPLM/A had to work hard to destroy this relationship.

The memories of the SPLM/A wars with Nuer communities in early 1980s and 1990s create a lot of destructions and these memories are so deep in the minds of those who witnessed them. The Nuer people were subjected to terror and starvation to the point that they have to exchange their cattle for food, blankets and other relief supplies. A Nuer man would rather die than seeing his cow being taken by another man. A young man who witnessed the incidents gave the following account:

"One time the SPLM/A army made a major assault in a small village called Liet Nyaruaach near Malual Ga-hoth, Upper Nile region, the attack happened at around 03:00 am. The army round up the whole village and started killing as much as they could, the fire was opened discriminatory, men, women, elderly and young children, the attack lasted for six hours from 3 to 9am. After SPLM/A soldiers left the whole village was like a pool of blood which had broken loss. When the assessment was done by the nearby village members on the situation of the village, almost all people were killed with the exception of few individuals who escaped for their lives and what the people found was a small child sitting in between her parents who were already dead, crying and was breast feeding from her dead mother who does not respond to her cry."

It was a terrible scene and people could not believe it. The situation which was done by their own sons who claimed that they are fighting for their liberation from Jalaba (Arabs), I only recall this through the chorus of the SPLA in a simple Arabic that goes as follows:

> I quote "Ketiba Bilpam manydu rahama shala abuk adiu Thalga" Loosely translates "Bipam Battalion has no Mercy, even your Father Give Him a bullet shot".

"I still have nightmares about this incident," he said. Here is the true mind-set of the SPLM/A movement towards the people of South Sudan. The majority said it clearly that during the graduation of soldiers after training, the Commander-in-Chief (C-in-C) would repeat the same instructions to the army raising his AK–47 and telling them, "this AK–47 is your Mom, your Dad, your wife and is everything to you want; so you are an Orphan, your Mom, Dad and your family is SPLM/A, Oyee, Oyee!" The movement brainwashed young people completely and subjected them to hatred towards their own people. This was a simple reason which everyone should pay no allegiance to any person rather than the C-in-C whom to them not less than a god".

Creating Differences within the Communities

The differences were created by the SPLM/A through disregard of human-rights and traditional values. There are ethical values that guide the individual within the community, however, within the SPLM/A disrespect and disloyalty are encouraged to promote rebellious attitudes. The communities were seen as the backward and need to be given guidance as part of the liberation agenda. As a result to address these dissatisfactions it resort into creating false differences within the communities that co-exist for many years, the Nuers and Dinka would portrayed each other. A Dinka is a traitor, a cheater and money lovers who can only sell the people of South Sudan to Jalaba (Arabs) in exchange for food and money. And Equatorian ethnic groups are cowards who abundant the struggle for the exchange of relief in the refugee camps. A picture up-to this moment still exists, and supported by the amount of corruption within the movement where resources are controlled by the leaders; they do not differentiate the private and public resources.

All the Nuer soldiers fall under the category of either Nyagad (Militias) or non-confirmed (not a real SPLA soldier) one of the Nuer artists composed a song:

I, quote *"Tameh chi mal ku ben chi yiou ben cha ney ngich cha ney chak chiot choalke ney ni not confirm-eeh! Not confirm enane moh ram chak je baguiy ekuoth wei"*

"Loosely translated, "Now peace has come and we are not recognized instead we are called not confirmed, this not confirmed that you see; we pray that the one who created it will be seen by God of this Nation."

The Dinka have the upper hands in the movement and are portrayed as the sole protectorate of the South, putting them above others, while in fact they were only exploiting these communities. But if you take a careful look you will find many Dinka communities were not in good term with the leadership, except those of Bor Dinka which claimed that "Kerbino Kuanyin Bol shot the first bullet in Bor town and Garang being their Son and educated give them a pride over other communities forgetting that the first bullet was shot by Any-nya II in Akobo by Gen. Vincent Kuany, Gen. Gordon Koang Benpiny and Aguet Awan in 1973-1975. These gentlemen remained in the bush until they were rejoined by others in 1983 when the SPLM/A was declared. Aguet Awan was later apprehended and sentence to death through military court in 1976.

System based on Security of the Few

The root cause of all crises in SPLM/A was the use of force to deal with political opponents. Many African dictators used this method to frustrate democracy which is badly needed by the African people. The South Sudan neighbors, Uganda and Sudan are good examples; Presidents Museveni, of Uganda was a mentor to late Garang, while Omar Bashir of Sudan who has spent over thirty years in power had been providing guidance to President Kiir to lead this new nation. Adding to Mesveni's evil tricks, the baby (South Sudan) mastered very quickly and learned how to flask his muscles doing what his big brother, Garang was doing, adopted by Kiir and group to make sure that whoever is seen as challenging his power base had to be taught a lesson. In December, 15, 2013 over 20,000 Nuer civilians were murder within three days and created internally displaced of 2 million people with a very short time.

"We know perfectly what conditions the majority of South Sudanese are facing Today, many people are killed, women, children and many elderly people. My daughter was burned inside her home with new born baby," came a voice of an elderly lady who spoke to me (Julia) on the phone in the UNMISS camp the evening of February 17, 2013 in Juba a month after the crisis.

It with this sadness many middle-age South Sudanese women have so many droughts in relation to this historic moment of their society; if they will ever build a nation. With just only three years of our independence, instead of celebrating the said freedom, we became to share a kind of fear of our lives; people ran for their lives, whisper in hiding places behind the bushes or hiding in the UN camps. Places where they used to be kept away by wild animals or by the UN heavy security are now their save heavens for the large sections of citizens. These places are now the hiding areas for so many people from all work of lives, MPs, constitutional post holders, civil servants, women and children, elderly and vulnerable groups, you name it, just because they belong to certain ethnic groups.

The majority of South Sudanese citizens thought that the ruling party (SPLM/A) or the government was for the people can become so bad and use its well know methods, it turns to become a killer and mobilizing one ethnic group against the other. The country in which people pay so dearly through the lives of love ones, and a long awaiting an expensive dream of progress, prosperity and freedom, ended being a tool to oppressed and harassed; journalists and western educated or well-trained individuals are the target. These groups of people are being censorship, kept out of prosperity and freedom they all dream off. Because, simply they are seen as carrying with them the wild idea of democracy and should be considered as they are enemy of the state. For the citizens this cannot just be comprehendible, but have sadness just to see their country being run by ignorance and group simple minded tribal military officers.

What good does it do for a few to enjoy and celebrate scarifies that were contributed by so many people who brought this nation? The concepts of freedom of speech by the citizens and a right to question to those who claim to be leaders have become a sin. Many people believed that they have a right to express their feelings to what they have seen, written, or said on the news, to question the intentions of those who want power to lead and to lead them for what? Where are the peace dividends so the citizens can believe them?

The citizens have a right to ask the wisdom of those who are in power and those seeking the power. They want them to listen to their inner voices or even see how much less embrace those leaders are today in eyes of so many South Sudanese and worldwide. The nation of South Sudan who has taken its pride among the world nations in July 9, 2011 has just become a laughingstock worldwide, because "Is it Leadership, stupid"! As South Sudanese search for answers to their painful saga through generations and no leader ever come closer to Garang's idea of New Sudan as solution to Sudan problem (Deng 2013). But many citizens know that it was Garang who set the stage of these incompetent leaders in the SPLM/A (Amon 1994).

It is with sadness that many citizens' tears seem not to be stopping rolling down their chicks seeing their people going through the same suffering which they endured for 50 years through the generations under the Islamic rule. Citizens are threatened, harassed or even lose their lives because they wanted to point out or questions things that were going wrong, those things that were threatening their lives and survival or simply they want services or quest for democracy, human rights and rule of law.

The majority of citizens have come to know now the country do not belong to the people as they thought because people cannot give opinions, raise issues of concerns or just demonstrate rational thinking then they become suspects. In many cases people are killed, cut-off or terrorized in the name of the security. Whose security and secure what? It is the warlords and cronies' security, the few chosen ones. Those who think they fought in the liberation. The towns in South Sudan have become war zones. The SPLM/A commanders move around with the mounted military army tracks recklessly through towns without obeying traffic rules. Those who are unlucky get hit and die as the law will never grant those rights.

On December 15, 2013, the definition of the security became very clear and was put in place. The presidential security guards known as Tiger, Dotku Beny and Mathiang Anyoor, all young men from the Dinka are from Awiel and Waarp states; they were ordered by the President that the J/day (Juba Day) is here. The plan was to eliminate the leader, Dr. Riek Machar; who led the group and called the December 6, 2013 press conference that demanded internal SPLM reforms, the time has come to teach him a lesson and not to get away with it, he need to be eliminated. The J/day was a payback for the 1991, the same demand Machar did and this should be done without any mistakes. Those who supported idea should also be arrested as soon as Riek Machar is finished. "Get to the house former Vice President and make sure no one leaves the house, we must smoke him out; the order goes", said one man who was a member of the presidential guards who refuse to use his name.

According to African Union Report 2014 and also stated by Gen. Mach Paul, the national security section under Gen. Akol Koor, Gen Duoth Guet of external security and plus the only trusted men were Generals Marial Changuong, Mangar Buong were in charge of the Presidential Guards, the Tiger Battalion were in control of Khor William, Gen. Garang Mabil for Mangateen. The ring leaders of the operations were led by Gen. Malong Awan, deputized by Gen. Salva Mathok Gengdit for Amarat neighborhood, Gen. Bol Akot for Gudele and Mia Saba neighborhoods, the Jieng Council of Elders and the President himself. His advisors, the Jieng (Dinka) Council of Elders, led by Ambrose Ring Thiik, Aldo Ajo and Joshua Dau were kept inform of the progress of the operation. On December 15, the majority of demobilized Dinka government officials with military background were given orders to put on their uniforms and report to Bilpam, the military Head Quarter.

Salva Mathok is a relative of the President and Gen. Bol Akot has been identified in many reports as a civilian who led militia at the time of massacres and whom Kiir later gave a senior rank in the army. The report goes on to quote the Minister of Defense Kuol Mangang as saying that a militia loyal to Salava Kiir kwon as Rescue the President (Dut Ku Beny in Dinka) "killed most people in Juba from December 15th to 18th." According the Minister of Defense and other witnesses described the forces as "personal army", which the President allegedly recruited and based at his private farm at Luri village seven miles near west of Juba Town.

Then the plan went wrong, Dut Ku Beny and Mathing Anyoor took the matter in their own hands. They took to streets and house to house killing any Nuer they found. The army tank that was send to demolish the V. P. house could not move faster enough to get to the house on time before the Dr. Reik left his home. When the guards got to the house, they did make sure that the house was demolished, 36 body-guards of Dr. Riek were killed. So did many incidents were Nuer civilians who were intentionally flash-out of their houses in Juba that night, follow by the other towns, Bentieu, Bor, and Malakal. Some Agar Dinka soldiers were also killed because they bare the same traditional marks with Nuer. The whole operations got out of hands and Juba became a killing field.

While the citizens were wandering to what has happened, the government search of would be the right story to shared. Finally, the story coup attempt surfaced. And the leadership gave order to detain Riek's supporters, those who participated in the press conference on the

December 6, 2013 before they get away. They were arrested under the pretext of coup attempt and they must answer to these charges.

It was not too long before the wisdom of Professor Nyaba, in February 2014 who broke the inside story that awaken the whole wide world, that there was no coup d'état but the President using the power of the state to deal with his political opponents who sawn their indentation to challenge him in the party leadership and the upcoming election in 2015. 'Whoops! a coup?' The cat is out of the cage.

The story of murdering of thousands of civilians is something that Kiir thought off for a very long time since the interim period of CPA, but he couldn't hide his actions which sent so much evidences that he had to find ways to cover-up the bad situation he had created. Professor Mahmood Mandani, a member of the AU Commission who authored a separate opinion on the Inquiry report stated, "The target violence was organized by leadership, not spontaneous. It was directed from the center."

Other testimonies in the report, however, point more to the role of organized forces in the killings rather than the so-called private army. Article 812 of the commission of Inquiry report concludes, "The evidence thus suggests that these crimes were committed pursuant to or in furtherance of a State policy. The method under which these crimes were committed proves the 'widespread or systematic nature' of the attacks. The evidence also shows that it was an organized military operation that could not have been successful without concerted efforts from various actors in the military and government circles. But state authorities continue singing a song of a repeated lie can become real. Keep repeating, it is a coup d'état, it is a coup; so that the government can justified the reason of killing incent civilians, that those who were killed were not civilians but those who fought in the coup operations were killed. Their method was similar to what the Nazis used during the World II,

"If you tell a lie big enough and keep repeating it, people will eventually come to believe it". Joseph Goebbels, Nazi propaganda Minister.

But the world didn't buy the story; only the little minded people were buying this story. The whole world waited as they watch government telling their side of the story, while many people were being displaced and many lives being lost (Nyaba 2014). The whole of planning started since early 2012 when the 15,000 militia were recruited and brought to Juba without knowledge of the Chief Staff of the organized forces General James Hoth Mai who happen to a Nuer. In September 28th to 30th, these militias were given orientation to know their locations. They were posted for two days in different locations as if they were cleaning Juba Town.

One of young man who was a member did provide an evident during interview, "They were not part of the SPLA; they were not part of Police or national security forces but part of a private army which trained to protect the President. He also stated, "The fight in 'Qiada' the Army Head Quarter was just to provoke the already plan to take place. It was just only a signal for this militia to start their work." Another witness says, "After orientation these were immediately told to be prepared for the signal," when the fighting started on December 15, 2013, these guys were now deployed and they did the killing, so it was a deliberate, it was something planned for a long time."

Social Delinquency and Recklessness

According to Neil Blandford and Bruce Jones (1995) who wrote about the atrocities in the Nazi Germany that, "described by teachers as a bit of a dreamer', Hitler because the monstrous dictator who manipulated the minds of the masses and caused the death of millions. The genocide of the Jews was one of the most cold-blooded acts the world has never seen, with men, women, children slaughtered as the "Final Solution'.

SPLM/A commanders failed to learn from the world history, their past and refused to revisit its vision if it really conforms with the view of the people of South Sudan. This lack of direction made many citizens and some high profile in the South Sudan both in politics and communities fell-out from their ranks and give-up their ties with the movement. Many politicians who do not want to be part of Khartoum Government decided to live in exile rather than joining the movement. Those who tried to speak their minds were locked end-up, being accused as traitors or wanting to over throw the leadership. SPLM/A policy was not questionable because of they believe that whatever come from leadership was considered sanction by truth. So the 1991 rebellion has to happen for there was no way in the world where a human being can lead without being question and does not accommodate others ideas. Queries on issues of concern were taken as an insult to the leadership intelligence's and it was punishable by death. Most of tiny educated class was killed; approximately two-third of the population fled the movement. In addition to its infamous cruelty and madness, the movement was characterized by weak administration ceased to faction and the population survived at barely subsistence level.

Although, the majority of experienced South Sudanese joined SPLM/A, well-educated with experience in the government of Sudan and well known individuals were all ignored. The leadership never takes any advice from them instead opt to prune them and filter them out as unwanted and calling those spoilers to the Movement. If anyone joins the movement they have to go through re-education for them to be considered a member.

The evil ones are too knowledgeable in their ways for the last three decades, the SLM/A was the only strong liberation movement in South Sudan. But its monopoly on liberation brought corruption in the movement. It sanctioned merciless killings and anyone who stands in their way was ruthlessly eliminated. It exterminated as heretics all who dared question it edicts about their world and life. And its members amassed immense wealth by looting the communities and state resources at free will. The unknown gun-man usually responded with enthusiasm to anyone who demands the corruption accountability in the country. The urban and rural areas become unsafe and trembling for fear of unknown gunman. Every night there are four to five murdered bodies discovered, live goes on, business as usual, it is a security work.

SPLM/A's recklessness brought the crisis of the December 15, 2013 and it is attributed to its failure to recognize that building a nation and leading a guerrilla movement are two different things. The tools that were used in running the movement are different from the tools that are needed now to run the nation. Another thing SPLM/A members miss is that an elected president has to be question by the electorates and can be criticized by his subjects because they hold him/her responsible for what he/she promised them during elections, and therefore he/she in turn accountable to the people.

As one time stated by the former Deputy Speaker of the National Assembly of Sudan, Hon. Atem Garang that, 'building the nation needs different tools than running a liberation movement.' What the SPLM/A leaders don't understand is that the appeal of democracy lines in these principles, according to Ostorm 1988 who stated that, first, refusal to accept in principle any conception of the political system/order/rule other than that generated by "the people themselves". Second, democracy is a mechanism that gives legitimacy on political decision when they stick to proper principles, rules and mechanisms of participation, representation and accountability. Third, democracy has been re-celebrated worldwide (and in our traditional way of life) as a way of containing the powers of elites who run the government of any country, of mediating among completing individuals and collective projects and rendering key political decisions accountable and it is a means to offer a basis for tolerating and negotiation differences. Fourth, Democracy does not presuppose agreement on diverse values; rather, it suggests a way of relating values to each other and of leaving the resolution of value conflicts open to participants in a public process, subject only to certain provisions protecting the shape and form of the process. We can than argue that, democracy is the answer to all questions far from it-but that, when adequately clarified and given a chance to test, democracy can be seen to lay down a program of change in and through which pressing, substantive issues will receive a better opportunity for deliberation, debate and resolution than they would under alternative (e.g. dictatorship) regimes.

These above principles we mentioned here are not part of the SPLM/A concepts and do not conform to the only concept they understand (one-man show) the power to control. This became the only tradition in which things are run, those who questioned the leadership were called disgruntle politicians or soldiers (Nyaba 2014). The system and those who led it had become good in creating terms and names to distort others people images. A book was written right after crisis tilted, "A First Fail Coup by Dr. Machar" written by the government of South Sudan, provides material worth reading. It is well-crafted carefully in response to Riek, Pagan and Rebbeca de Mabior, the widow of John Garang for their aspirations for leadership. The SPLM/A members have learned the same style of Museveni's politics which he uses against his rivalries in Uganda. Museveni is a master in manipulating the political space by terrorizing his political opponents. Those who had tried to out seat Museveni find it very difficult because he had mastered the art of political assassination to narrow political space and character assassination of his political opponents. Those who are Museveni's rivalries are either charge with treasons, rape, corruption or other immoral behaviors; they have to be deal with because they are enemies of the state, the case of the members of Democratic for Change Party (New Nation 2011).

When president Museveni was invited to attend the South Sudan 2nd Independence Celebration, he loudly in his speech advised President Kiir to carry the stick in one hand, the AK-47or the sword on the other hand. Telling Kiir that whoever tried to temper with leadership he must use these weapons wisely. He should hit the one who is not so dangerous with the stick and cut the head of the one who is more dangerous with sword, (Juba Monitor 2012). This is not different from the method use by South Africa partied regime over the majority blacks population.

The hallmarks of pillage and plunder are strongly visible in running the political affairs of South Sudan. Where villages were raged, youth who were operating under communal were given free hand to commit enormous atrocities. Killing and demeaning elders, rape and forcible taking teen girls as "war wives", desecrating or destroying religious shrines and humiliating and leaching eminent individuals in the community chattered acceptance of the multi-ethnic South Sudan (Gen. Tot Wei).

The narrowing of the political space had left the South Sudanese struggling to find themselves. The debate among the South Sudanese has been focusing on the principles of autonomy (federal system), according to them the autonomy is a principle for the demarcation legitimate power; it expresses a concern with the specification of the foundations of democracy consent. These can be elaborated as follows: (a) the nation that persons should enjoy equal rights and obligations in political framework which shapes their lives and opportunities means, in principle, that, they should enjoy equal autonomy-that is, a common structure of political action in order individual and collective can pursue interests freely; (b) the concepts of "rights" connotes entitlements to pursue action and activity without the risk of arbitrary of unjust interference in people's lives; (c) the people should be free and equal in the determination of the conditions of their own lives, means that they should be able to participate in a process of debate and deliberation, open to all on free and equal basis, about matters of pressing public concern; (d) constitutional rule: the principle of autonomy specifies both that individuals must be "free and equal" and that "majority" should not be able to impose themselves on others. There must always be institutional arrangements to protect the individual's or minority's position (V. Ostorm 1988). So the cry of the majority of South Sudanese had been on the constitutional reforms so that to keep the hands of dictators off their lives, but the dictators had taken the country as their own property. Those who have power determine governing structure.

Public Interest and Organization of Society

By becoming socially involved with other people, communicating with them, and cooperating in crucial tasks, an individual extends his understanding, starts to thinks in universal terms to embrace interests in the larger community, and has concerns for those with whom he/she lives, works and cooperates with. It is within such as arrangement that the term "public" interests make sense. The term "public" embraces any result of the extension of an individual that is part of "open social relationship" (Simon, Herbert 1973).

The postulate of an open social relationship excludes all cases of combinations and conspiracies started with intention of taking advantage of a combined effort. They then create special privileges and secure the privileges for the members of the group at the expense of others. This postulate was no part of foundations of SPLM/A ideology, if such a conspiratorial group seizes control of the movement, understood as a monopoly of control over the means of coercion, and with its use of coercion extends this monopoly to other domains of social life, it creates the worst kind of exploitation. Other groups cannot constrain it within the existing institutional framework.

The public realm is a hierarchy, in the sense used by Herbert Simon (1973), that, although the first extension of self-include the family and the peer group, others will, if they occur at all embrace wider social entities such as voluntary associations, if they occur at all embrace wider social entities such as voluntary associations, clubs, unions, religious denominations, local communities, a country, and eventually the world as a whole.20 Family and peer group loyalties are natural and universal because families and peer groups are found everywhere and at all times; in joining them an individual exercises little freedom of choice.

In most circumstances the same applies to religious affiliations. Of crucial importance are, therefore, those institutions and social relations that an individual can create or join on his/her own initiative as long as they provide the welfare of the larger group.

According to Ostrom 1988, stated that public life is possible only when fundamental human freedoms are respected. But, in order for public life to appear at all, the family peer groups, voluntary associations, and religious institutions must function in a way that strengthens universal moral and intellectual orientations. These preconditions of public life are recognized, for example, as a factor in shaping American pre-revolutionary political life; they might also be, in an opposite way, affecting the South Sudan People's Liberation Movement.

From this perspective, the public and the private are not necessarily exclusive and may be mutual reinforcing. That is, once an ethos develops is in the private domain that is enhancing the operational of the public domain, the condition for the development of the public domain is met. Any progress in the development of the public domain will in turn enforce the underlying values of the private. For example, the successful negotiation of a conflict of interest will enhance the probability that, if the conflict recurs, the parties would turn to negotiation and adjudication rather than to belligerence in settling it.

It is only when the community of understanding and the consensus about values and norms falters that a crisis of the public domain will occur. Absence of common understandings was the characteristic of movement before 1991, and perhaps, beyond. Then we should expect the reverse of the process described above: broader loyalties begin to shrink, the bounds of trust disappear, and values and norms become less universalistic and more particularistic. Eventually, individuals find protection in families and other informal groups, or in small political and cultural communities trying to impose their particular ethos on society.21 When society is unable, for various reasons, to maintain and defend the public domain, that is the institutional diversity which, with the underlying community of understanding, provides the basis for integration, corruption sets in. On the level of individual administrative or political roles this takes the form of using a public office for the sake of person enrichment or aggrandizement.

This is the point we want to make by saying that socialism gains power by encouraging conflict. The effects of personalization, increased predation, and repression have been disengagement and other manifestations that offer the possibilities for the survival of individuals and communities in the south Sudan. The policy of terror became the order of the day and humans have to learn their ways around to survive among the evil genius, control them and set the agenda of livelihood.

The process of disengagement from SPLM/A

The process of disengagement with movement was clearly demonstrated in the following ways: the breakaway of Nasir Group to form a different liberation front of the SPLM/A; the organization of SPLM/A – United by Nasir Group, Equatorian Group led by Late Joseph Oduho; and the Barh El Ghazal Group led by Commander Kerobino Kwanyin; other groups, Anuak, Murle, Toposa, and Latuka fighting against SPLM/A instead of northern Sudanese and facilitating the capturing of Pachalla, Pibor, Kapoeta, and Torit Towns; a return to the way of life of the people, at least in the Upper Nile Region, in the use of indigenous conflict resolution mechanisms; accepting refuge in the neighboring countries by fighting men; increased number of young and middle age persons accepting to go for survival among different peoples in the southern Sudan and has also shown to the SPLM/A what people can do when human beings are treated as means to some individual's end. The price of inequality is being paid by many South Sudanese today. Below is a story told one of the young man who witness the incident when SLPM/A came to the village, people started running and hiding.

"Guandit Guandit chu ring chi ney gor ni ji. Ah gaatkah cha duth wuurah mi wa yen ah chop, bi yen ha le pal."

Loosely translated "Old man, Old man, don't run we are not looking for you. Oh my sons I already ran, when you catch up with me you may leave me."

Looking into this simple story, according to the majority of South Sudanese, one can realize that there is a serious destruction and the breakdown of communities' values for it had never happened that young people would be chasing an old man. If there is a war, small children, women and old men are not to be harm, for they are protected by values and traditions especially among the Nuer and Dinka communities. Also, the issue of raping cannot be heard for it is a taboo within the Nilotic communities whatever the case may be, during war time between Nuer and Dinka, sometimes they raided young people, women and girls and they will have to be protected until the traditions and rituals are preform before a man could touch a captured lady when they bring the captives home.

SPLM/A, disregards these important values and traditions that for so long were the basic foundation of our communities as Africa; most of the laws are not written, rather than they are being embodied within the traditions and values, therefore it could have been important for the movement take the lead to respect these values rather destroying them. Moreover, since the inception of the movement in 1983, tribal wars started and many communities became enemies and the gap between Nuer and Dinka became very grave and widen than ever and had reached its peak with the current crisis.

Since 2005, the formation of government had not change from the formation of movement in 1983, the Judiciary, the Central Bank, the ministries of Defense and Interior, Chief Security, Chief Military Inelegancy, Chief of General Staff of the Army, Police chief, Inspector General of Police and its two deputies are all control by one group. This is just an example in the security sector in a country inhabited by more than sixty tribes that only one group can provide the security for all other groups.

Therefore, all these wars fought in South Sudan since 1983 are interlinked with the philosophy of the movement on creating chaos to control the environment in order to find a space to do business as usual and the citizens are suffering from war trauma and not benefiting from the services that should have been provided by the government.

Development of the Syndrome of Asymmetry

In its Manifesto (July 31, 1983), the SPLM was to be the all-powerful initiator of an action program. The SPLA was to serve as the instrument, and the southern society was to be the object to be molded. Garang leadership of the SPLM/A translated this image into an institutional structure that assigned no power to the other SPLM/A members who are holding leadership positions. The relationship between the SPLM/A with Nuer, Equatorian ethnic groups and other cultural groups was asymmetrical relationship; this is shown in all aspects where contacts occur. It is illustrated her in four major areas: political, economic, social and judicial.

In the political arena there was a lack of connection between priorities of the SPLM/A and the needs and aspirations of the people in the southern Sudan. Political asymmetry usually refers to the fact that ordinary people cannot function in any sense as rulers-ruled have <u>all</u> authority. That leadership "clearly understands". From this basic political asymmetry, other follows.

In its economic life, the village people or the rural people have been prevented from cultivating or trading in the SPLM/A controlled area. This situation has resulted in a permanent shortage of food supplies and other goods. In the domain of social communication, there is a lack of correspondence between the content and the language of messages disseminated by the newspapers and radio (owned and operated by the movement) and the opinions, attitudes, interests, and linguistic conceptualizations of most of the southern Sudanese. Justice takes the form of what Kaminski has called the "prosecution's court." Where the prosecutor has more weight in the court than the defense, while at the stage of investigation, the position of the prosecutor is in the turn weaker than that of the investigating officer (Kaminski, 1992). 44 In the SPLM/A an accused before the Military Martial Court stand little chance of being found innocent, especially non-Dinka (Oduho, 1992).22; Wantok et al, 1992). Interests taken in account are first of all those that matter: the security of the leadership, the armed forces, and collective wealth of the ruling, commander class. Other interests and concerns are a secondary, such as building civil institutions, a peace process, and finding solutions to the civil war merit attention only sporadically when situation is critical. When face-to-face discussions and democracy threaten or were perceived to be threaten ruling commanders class interests, these avenues to a solution were attacked.23 The institutional design problem is, then, not only one of error detection but also one of error correction: the system is opaque, and behind the veil of secrecy are hiding powerful groups whose survival depends on their being able to maintain their lack of accountability to the southern Sudanese public. The SPLM/A's ability to correct its errors is limited but also, within limits, it is an error-amplifying arrangement. They kept their position on creating an environment that is intimidating and violence. The leadership of the SPLM/A was very good in making all the population to live in fear and concentrating on insulting others leaders to destroy them.

The relationships among the SPLM's leaderships, the SPLA, and the peoples in southern Sudan are those of the relationships is to maximize of control by SPLM's leadership over commanders class and commanders class over society, which is object to be transformed. This situation implies an inherent conflict between the SPLA and disregard the southern population entirely only when they strip members of the different groups of ability to organize themselves for action. Community organizations were seen as a collective force towards leadership and must be destroyed.

A passive, atomized society has certain disadvantages for the SPLM/A because passivity and indifference do not foster purposive activity and voluntary cooperation. With the decline of civic ability in strength, cultural and military spheres, the SPM/A leadership and commander's class were forced to recognize the importance of self-motivated activity and cooperation for their political survival. Unfortunately, this realization has led them to a dead end. The suppression of the southern people resulted from the basic design of the "Soviet" type regime of SPLM/A and not from errors in policy, so the current position of the SPLM/A's leadership is based upon the continuation of this socially alienating arrangement. When the institutional structure changes; their position will change as well either for better or worst. They have no other justification for their privileged position besides Marxist-Leninist doctrine and the survival of the error-amplifying system of order of the current SPLM/A.

CHAPTER FIVE

The Emergence of an Alternative Liberation Movement

THE VARIOUS LANGUAGE groups in the southern Sudan are deeply ingrained in their habits and traditions. They function well so long as the central organizing principles of traditional ways can be maintained. The reason for this is because all social orders are embedded in the shared understanding of a people. As indicated in the earlier section of this report, a lack of understanding of the principles used by these groups in organizing their ways of life is an important problem in the constitutional order in SPLM/A. The ideas to which people have recourse, the language they use, and the way they marshal activities are the key foundations upon which their continuing existence and development are built. The period after the establishment of the SPLM/A has been and still is a period of endless imitation an experimentation, applying pet notions from the former Soviet bloc with a view to transforming the southern Sudan movement into a socialist one. While the governance system of the liberation movement was marked by institutional weakness ad failures, there was little, if any, attempt to search for alternatives.

The commitment of the SPM/A to Marxist-Leninist – types institutional order has simply replicated the problem of governmental over-centralization. It is grounded on the principle of dominance. Struggles to gain power over others may be the predominant mode of organization of the Sudanese liberation movement. Such a goal is bound to fail. The SPLM/A (United) was a reaction against the guiding principle of dominance, however, challenges of lack of resources weaken SPLM/A – United and scramble over the leadership, Riek and Lam went different way and the Dinka members, Teler Deng, Deng Chol Alaak and Deng Tiel went back to Garang for mercy, while Kawaj Makuei and Atem Gualdit join Karabino and went their own way. The Equatorians led by General Martin Kenyi and Dr. Tiepolo Ochang created Equatorian Defense Force (EDF), which also was anti-Garang. The group moved to Khartoum to the Khartoum Peace Agreement in 1996. Other groups were SPLM/A Bahr el Ghazal Group, the Bor Group led by those of General Arok Thon with all join in (KPA) in 1997 (Young 2006). The only man who remains with his words was Adok Nyaba who kept the light of South Sudan shining through his pen. He kept telling the story of bad governance and leadership that had failed the people of South Sudan.

The SPLM/A Factions

The split in SPLM/A was the result mainly of opposition to the centralization generated by a Marxist-Leninist institutional order and abuses of human rights.27 In addition to the lack of flexibility in the movement and the human rights abuses, there was no clear vision of what the war was all about. This intra-SPLM/A conflict in one sense represents a renegotiation of what the civil war is about. In another sense, the disputes represent a reaffirmation of the reality of the fundamental theory of civil society underlying the political order in the southern Sudan and the importance of attempts to restore respect of indigenous ways of life. The failure of the ideology let to failure of the movement. According to John Young, 2007 stated that the Sudan People's Liberation Movement (SPLM) could not stand to the task because their ideology was not clear to the people of southern Sudan who were fighting for self-determination. The concept of the

New Sudan in which the SPLM/A fighting for is far off the mind of a common South Sudanese. The common person wanders why they should fight to liberate the Northern Sudan?

The Sudan People's Liberation Movement/ Army (Mainstream)

The SPLM/A Mainstream continue to be led by John Garang who is from Dinka of Kongor, Jonglei Province, Upper Nile Region.28 Since its inception in the South, Garang's intentions were to achieve the liberation of the whole Sudan from the minority Arabs and to establish a socialist government for the whole Sudan. This sound good to the Pan Africanist making Garang the true son of Africa, but this does not ring the bell in the ear of common South Sudanese who is suffering in the hands of the Arabs.

Garang creates alliance with The National Democratic Alliance (NDA), one of the northern Sudan's opposition movements. Simply because NDA opposed the National Islamic Front, one cannot assume that, if it were to take over the reins of power in Khartoum, its control would create a condition sufficient for the emergence of a productive civil society in the Sudan.29 The bonds that unite individuals and groups in NDA and SPLM/A-Mainstream have a strongly moralistic, negative character. NDA was trying to use the SPLM/A as spring-board to power. A civil society requires a positive vision, an ability to cooperate in construction-not only in destruction, a respect for other persons that precludes the development of a zero-sum game. A civil society reflects principles of socialization implied by the acts of being civil and partaking in a civilization.

The NDA were composed of the SPLM/A, The Omma Party, Democratic Union Party (DUP), Communist Party, and a few other smaller parties. These parties are opposed to the holding of a multi-option referendum in the South and among other marginalized communities resident in the northern Sudan, such as the Nuba and the people of southern Blue

Nile region. At times, John Garang, leader of the SPLM/A-Mainstream faction that is a member of the NDA, talks of con-federal relationships with the North. The language used in reference to the concept of confederation requires clarification. Many political scientists agree that an essential attribute of a government is the capacity to enforce law. A confederation, as traditionally conceived, could not meet this defining criterion for a government (Montesquieu 1966: 180-182). A confederate assembly, which depends upon member republics to enforce law, is not a government in the proper signification of the word (Ostrom 1992:44-455). Its resolution is not binding as rules of law but constitute mere recommendations to member states. According to Alexander Hamilton a confederation is a government of governments. To him this is an absurdity. This reference is contained in essays 15 and 16 of the Federalist (Ostrom 1992). The Nuba, Abiei Dinka and peoples of southern Blue Nile are not part of the South Sudan according to the 1954 demarcated boundaries, but the majority of Abiei Dinka and some members of the Nuba have been supportive of the liberation movement with the people that they will find their freedom as well. A united New Sudan is a good product to sell in the north and other parts of Sudan.

By 2005, however, most of the prominent Nuba leaders in SPLM/A-Mainstream have become disillusioned with the movement. These leaders have joined the movement seeking autonomy for their area within the united Sudan.30 They feel they are betrayed by a movement that seeks self-determination only for the south. The demand for referendum was presumed to be equivalent to a call for separation of the South. The outcome of a multi-option referendum would, however, depend crucially on what option were allowed.

John Young (2007), stated that while there is no doubting the confusion caused by the SPLM/A's early filtrating with a primitive Marxism and much more the formulation of the New Sudan ideology, liberation movements beyond the south have also failed to produce strong ideologies and as a result have contributed to the present state of disunity in the northern Sudan. The confusion begins with the leaders of the liberation movements who typically have a history of shifting from the ideological orientation to another over the years, thus leaving the impression that the endorsement of an ideology is not the product of serious study and identification with its principles, but is based on a consideration of whether it will be a suitable vehicle to advance personal interests.

For 21 years, John Garang managed to manipulate the minds of so many people, tell them what they want to hear. When he was meeting the South Sudanese he was for secession and when with the northern Sudanese he was for unity. A well calculated message that stance seems to have been tailored to please whoever come in contact with John Garang. He and his followers stressed that they were fighting for the south, that it was a struggle of dispossessed Africans against the Arabs, and that it was a war to free the south (Rolandsen, Oystein 2005).

Ideological Objective of SLPM/A (under John Garang)

The first civil war was war of liberation of South. However, the second phase of the civil war in Sudan was more than a continuation of hostilities between North and South. It was a different kind of liberation struggle based on Pan African Socialist system. The Southern Sudan Liberation Movement/Army (SSLM/A), the Anya-nya had been fighting a regional war exclusively for the independence of Southern Sudan. On the other hand the Sudan People Liberation Movement/Army (SPLM/A) chose to fight for the liberation of all the Sudanese peoples from the regime in Khartoum. Garang strategy was to stop the South from thinking of itself as a victim trying to flee from the hands of a violent state and start believing in its own abilities to change the country (Yates 2012). On March 1985 he out lined his vision of a "New Sudan" on the six principles:

1. Establishment of democracy, social justice and human rights
2. Secular nationalism
3. Regional autonomy and/or federalism
4. Radical restructuring of political power

5. Balance regional development and
6. Eliminating institutional racism (Arabs vs Africans)

None of these principles was based on a singular southern belief. Garang based his struggle on ideological objectives that offered a vision of a better future to all the Sudanese people. He defined the aims of the struggle as redressing regional inequalities in the east, west, north and the south. He defined the enemy not as northerners, but as particular "family dynasties" and "political parties" controlled by certain families or religious sets who had monopolized power to the detriments of all Sudanese people. By refining the goals of the struggle for liberation, his vision of a "New Sudan" allowed the SPLM/A to build multiregional alliances against a common enemy. Garang believes that all the troubles of Sudan are cause by the state build on a single Arabic Islamic nationalism. It was confirmed by his popular quotes that, 'God created Arabs, Fur, Nuba, Nuer, Dinka and all 500 communities in Sudan, who is this man in Sudan to amend God creation? If this case is taken to God, I will win this case (wal alhah llah zim) in the name of Almighty creator." Although, there was no questioning about his logic on the challenging the government method of governance (Deng 2010) but his methods of running the liberation were being questioned.

The armed struggle and the political mobilization of the masses was seen as essential to the creation of a New Sudan, with the SPLM/A serving as the instrument of this transformation. Deng stated in his book (2009), "War of Vision" that, "The birth in 1983 of the SLPM/A as a politico-military organization furnishes the Sudanese revolutionary struggle with the armed component required to confront the armed custodian of the minority Arab clique rule." The government of Sudan terrorized civilian populations from the South, Durfur, Kordofan and the Blue Nile regions who responded to this call in big number made what could be a regional war between north and the south became a total war between the center and the periphery.

Then in 2005 the government singed a Comprehensive Peace Agreement with SPLM/A ushering in a return to the regional autonomy and promising to hold a referendum on Southern Sudan independence. NCP and SPLM/A agreed to share power offering John Garang the position of vice president in the government of Sudan and the presidency of the government of southern Sudan. Three weeks later, while returning from talks with president of Uganda, John Garang died in a helicopter crash on Saturday, July 30, 2005. He was replaced by his successor, Salva Kiir the deputy chairman of SPLM and chief of staff of the SPLA. Kiir is more inclined to secession than his predecessor. He quickly abandons Garang vision of a united Sudan, in 2009 addressing public and told them that their choice was between "voting for unity and being second-class citizen in your own country or voting for independence and be a free person in an independent country." This statement sat the stage for the referendum vote of the 99% for the independent of South Sudan.

The Sudan People's Liberation Movement/Army (United)

Discontent with Garang's leadership had led to the formation of breakaway groups in August 28, 1991. The Nasir Group, the Equatorian Group, and Bahr el Ghazal Group have allied themselves to form SPLM/A-United led by Riek Machar, a Nuer. The majority of the SPLA-United foot soldiers, however, were Nuer. It was strong in their homeland, the Upper Nile Region and part of Eastern Equatoria Region, the Tabosa and other groups who resisted the SPLA in their areas. Garang had never been broadly elected by, rather, had been chosen by a few officers. His leadership had been ruthless against dissident and had been responsible for terrible human rights against fellow southern Sudanese (Human right watch report 1995).

The Nuer resented the way they and other minority groups have been treated by the Dinka.31 As indicated in the early sections of this book, the ideology formulated by Garang was communist, and there was a close relationship with Mengistu's Ethiopia. Nuer could not identify with the principles underlying a Soviet-type organization. Garang had to rely on force to attempt to transform the southern Sudanese Liberation organization into a real socialist movement. Finally, the Nuer heartily supports the SPLM-United's objective of liberating the South, not liberating all of Sudan. They believe the Southern people should have the right to express their views in a multi-option referendum. They believe the overwhelming majority of the people would choose to have a separate independent state.

John Garang also had complained that SPLM/A-United of being in league with the Khartoum Government and receiving arms from Khartoum. This charge is strongly denied. Garang also has complained that SPLM/A-United was not really fighting the Sudan army. The SPLM/A-United admitted that it was not carrying out offensive war against the Sudan army because they do not have the capability to do so. Whatever weapons they have was to maintain the armed stalemate.

According to Commander John Luke, "the Dinka have all arms from the sources which used to support us when we were one." However, "they talk loudest but do very little fighting.32 "SPLM/A-United claims that it has been its members who have been carrying the burden of fighting the enemy since 1983. Since the breakaway, Garang has not captured a single town. Instead, he has lost most of the towns, such as Torit, Kapoeta, Yirol, Kaya, Bor, Pachalla etc, that were previously controlled by the SPLM/A. In Wal Duany's visit to the Upper Nile region controlled by the forces of the SPLM/A-United in September/ October 1993, he did not found the evidence that the Government of Sudan was supplying arms to the SPLM/A-United. His impression was that the forces of the United were poorly equipped. He did not, however, visit Eastern Equatoria where Commander William Nyuon operates. Further investigation of this charge was conducted and we were able to conform that at the beginning SPLM/A – Untied did get any support from the Sudan government and the charges dismissed entirely. The reality was that both factions were trying to survive, if there was a devil that can provide weapons, they will accept so that they over run each other out of the south. However, later through the years Wal found out that the Sudan Government develop interest and allied with SPLA-United to provide supports in the war against Garang. But the arms that were given were not enough to fight Garang but to keep him engaged; a good method of divide and conquered.

The difficulty in determining what SPLM/A was fight for a united Sudan or an independent south, existed to 2005 and had spread confusion among the northerners. The NDA does not share SPLM/A-United's interest on a referendum that would offer the possibility of independence for the South (Young 2005). The NDA would rather prolong the civil war than to see an independent South. This strategy of dividing the South is identical with the policy of the Government of the Sudan. The Government insists or prefers talking with each other of the Southern factions separately. The major towns in the south became the centers of mobilization, south Sudanese inside Sudan were more exposed to Islam and Arabic culture, those were outside were exposed to different cultures and the rural communities were left to their traditional cultures. The people of South became disconnect and the only thing that unites them was fight against the north. The north was also calculating, the longer the civil war lasts, the better the prospects for Arabicizing and Islamizing the South. This similarity of purpose on the part of the NDA and the GOS was not clearly recognized by the factions of the SPLM/A.

Organizing Principles of the SPLM/A-United

The Nasir Declaration of August 28, 1991 was the breakaway of group of officers who later became known as the Nasir Group of SPLM/A. The Nasir Declaration represented the culmination of a struggle over the principles of equality, justice, freedom of action, and self-administration and Marxist-Leninist top-down principles of institutional order in the light of failure to modify the constitution of order in the SPLM/A to accommodate the Nuer and other southern Sudanese conception of civil and military systems of governance.25

The way Nuer think of their life is reflected in the way they organize their social and military relationships.26 The presumption of equality before their Creator gives individual equal standing in the establishment of patterns of order. A non-hierarchical order is regarded as normal. The Nuer believes in a common creation and a commitment to the laws of their Creator. All Nuer are created by God and therefore they are all children of God. God has given <u>raan</u>, or each person's life and ability to think for themselves so that they can do certain things of their own to advance their interests and to glorify their Creator. There is the implication that the development of a group is primarily viewed as a process of mutual agreement of covenanting among individuals. This further implies that the Nuer constitution is an artifact made by people to achieve important tasks and things of value for themselves. Whenever such institutional arrangements are destructive to life and things of value, it is the right of the people to change or abolish such a system of institutional order.

The presupposition that all persons are created equal is grounded in Nuer religious tradition that all Naath (human beings) are fundamentally equal before their Creator. This Nuer tradition teaches that all people derive from a common parentage. There is thus reason to believe that there is a basic "similitude" of thoughts and passions that characterizes all human kind.

The development of social conventions that make a virtue of both justice and freedom of action derives from two elements: the concept of equality in relation to some transcendent order; and the possibility of achieving harmony in human affairs by choosing to order relationships in accordance with university rules that are conceived as God's law (Ostrom, 1991:58; Evans-Pritchard,1956). Individual differences exist but do not disprove the presupposition that all persons are created equal, that can also serve as a valid basis for the better ordering of relationships through just and equal laws. To regard one another as free and equal in some fundamental sense may be a better way of constituting the southern Sudanese liberation movement than to presume that everyone is un-free or equal. These organizing principles have separated the SPLM/A – United apart from the SPLM/A-Mainstream. However, Riek did not learn from Garang's mistakes which later lead to disintegration of his forces and he ended up rejoining Garang in 2000. This haunted him up to his second rebellion in 2013 when he got forced out by Kiir and had to run for his life. The challenge for Riek is how he convinces the poplars that he can be a change leader that can lead the reforms in South Sudan. This is a tough mission in the miss of grave sufferings and poverty that enclave the nation.

When Kiir's trusted evil genius members dream-up of genocide of the Nuers as his "final solution" for Machar's problem, he could have wish for no than General Paul Malong Awan and his tribal Jieng Council of Elders. With cold-blooded relish they became the most methodical mass murderers in time of South Sudan history, forever seeking improvements in their machinery for massacring an entire Nuer people. This was thought out as a lesson for Machar that the 1991 Bor massacre was not forgotten but paid back to him dearly while he is still alive. They logged their lethal efficiency with pride of obsequious civil servants including a few Nuers politicians who could not see the reality and shared their convictions that their efforts had been foiled by traitors (those Nuer soldiers who answered the cry of innocent citizens who scape the massacre of December 15, 2013). Some Nuer commanders along with anti-Machar tide politicians who saw nothing wrong in the motto that it is better to kill a few innocent Nuers and non-Dinkas than let one guilty party (Machar) escape.

The Nuer Indigenous Defense System

The Nuer has a well organize security system in which the art of war is part of socialization. Because they believe the uncertain of the nature are part of daily life. The defense of the homeland is paramount and a duty of all the members of society. This strong foundation gave the Nuer upper recognition over their neighbors during the British rule. The idea that the Nuer and to a lesser extent the Dinka, are more naturally warriors was provided by Evans-Pritchard writings. The competition over the water and pasture generated periodical cycles of conflicts between them. The system adopts new war skills from generation to generation. In late 1920s, the Eastern Nuer, Lou and Jekany were the first communities to introduce the modern war weapons, making them more powerful than their neighbors, the Dinka and the Murles.

The conceptions Nuer about their relationships with one another affects the way their defense system is organized. Individuals are presumed to be equal. This concept of equality is compatible with the development of active individual participation in the defense of a segment of Nuer society. The leaders of the liberation movement misunderstand the way people organized their life and how to mobilize local resources. Prichard (1934) also wrote extensively that the Nuer are great peacemakers because to them peace is define as life and it is projected in their greetings "maale" peace upon you. Dr. John Garang did not understand and so did many Dinka leaders who have not come to crisp that every Nuer is the product of hard upbringing deeply democratic society. The Nuer are good at negations, their understanding is that if you want to talk they will talk and if you want a fight they will be ready too (Evan-Prichard 1934). The lack of understand by the Dinka leaders generate the violence we seen today in South Sudan.

Ngundeng's Social Concept of Nation

Dr. Wal Duany describes in his book, "Neither Palaces nor Prisons" (Duany 2013), that Ngundeng Bong and his System of governance as hierarchy that example of Prophetic era. Ngundeng Bong politically is a unifier. He uses settlements and inter-communal relations to drive his unity messages. Placing the Mond (worship place) closer to the Gun and Mor Lou's boundaries was a great act of state man-ship and enhanced both his spiritual leadership as well as the unity among the people. His place of the *Mond* (worship) was permanent. His spiritual place was accessible to Jikeny and Gaawar, Laak and Thiang as well as

Dinka Padang. Ngundeng's rule represents the full expression of Nuer Nationalism-One Nation in one land under one God.

Ngundeng's political mission was based on promotion of peace among people, and the nation is not yet entirely atelier. He was making extensive contacts with other tribal leaders who were his neighbors. Treaties were signed and payments for mutual damage made. He began actual taxation: Cattle pay and/or labor in lieu of taxes and this was used for common good of the community. He began dividing the country into administrative districts by appointing officials at different levels of expertise. The people were enlisted for the public services and supervised by a central administration which Ngundeng or the prophet had appointed. There was a body of officials answerable to the prophet/leader. He developed young people through hierarchy making sure young people are train to take up the future leadership. The fact that Guek Ngundeng and Dual Dieu took over the leadership was Ngundeng's official's endorsement of young leadership that in fact a new class had come into being. It was also very important that under Ngundeng the priests assure appointment by prophet/leader and in this way all priests became loyal officials. These spiritual leaders are picked among the highly screened young people who come from good families and are moral and ethical rights.

Survival: how do we explain the survival of the Nuer as people? The explanation is not only the amazing persistence of the species, maintaining a continuous identity over thousands of years, but the consistence over time presentation, factionalism and survival. The usual explanation of the survival of the Nuer is related to the Nuer religion that makes it a tightly knit community able to transmit its values over generations. The massager (Dengion) position was a high capacity for cultural representation (Duany 1992, 2013, Douglas 1980).

No doubt but to reproduce one first has to survive. Wildavsky 1984 stated that constant Religion values and social practices cannot be used to explain a variable- a deputation to widely varying circumstances over the thousands of years. An insight is given by Hocart: "it may be in the evolution of institutions that shall find the key to the problem of adaptation of organisms generally..... seeking from it in ourselves {rather} then outside human society among animals and plants" (A.M. Hocart, 1970) : P 299) to direct this thrust, add W. Ross Ashby's "Law of Requisite Variety" it takes variety to cope with variety (Ashby, 1968: Ch 15.) (See Boyd and Campbell).

Disabilities of Regimes in Sudan can be explain in these four factors that has fatal political disabilities and this had enable South to break away from Sudan.

- Slavery: {Extreme Centralization) because master do not have to pay attention to slaves, slave societies are vulnerable {susceptible to} on the ground of ignorance (without participation in the societies' activities such as decision making person in this group cannot) leadership each running and this is paralleled key friend in capacity to initiate future event. When the (everybody who depends upon others repeats the mistakes).

- Anarchies became of level boundaries (No function and differentiation) they amount defunct themselves as source even through their permit information unless everyone agrees to play the game with the some rules. There are enough groups to recombine, the game goes on, but if there is a big group that will not let the other (smaller) play, it is over.

- Equities suffer from lack of excess of leadership. Either equities reject authority or to follow a leader who has to proof below that he is a perfect under to maintain their support and allegiance. Separation (keeping aloof) from society renders equities important, and confrontation may kill them. Preservation is the primary goal of the hierarchy. Once an order is given it must be carried out. Activities in various officials are coordinated. The hierarchy often slows to adapt to change condition; and when it does adapt, it does by over commuting the population to the new departure and becomes difficult to return to the original position. Where do we locate the secret of Survival of the Nuer People: It is imaginable that the structural weakness and environmental change combining to kill any type of regime. There are certain things a regime cannot do as condition the system cannot adapt. When the infallibility of the Master is challenged, or the rule of the unlimited transactions (prisoner) is abolished, or the equity splits, or the hierarchy becomes slugged, these regimes can an able (Wildvasky 1984: 230) but the Nuer People survived through the regime under they have not? The secret of survival lies precisely on avoiding commitment to a single type of regime. Nuer god has rule over hierarchy and anarchy but view equity and hierarchy as permissible. Since the two regimes have different disabilities and different strengths, one will survive whereas the other will not.

• A movable hierarchy is almost an empirical contradiction. In order to have specialization and division of labor, there must be a structure of a certain size. Being large in size and fixed in geography, therefore hierarchies can conceivably be wiped out with one blow. They are robust (Do have with it), but can be overturned by an unfriendly environment.

The majority of Nuer in the state of Sudan spear headed that the south should separate and become a different entity. The Nuer social system is very strong in assimilation of the people who are foreigners (non-Nuer) as long as those foreigners are not utterly hostile. This strong system of assimilation make the Nuer people believe that it is easier to assimilate a foreigner, then of your own people because of share values.

Small size of institution governance is a distinguishing mark of equity. Lack of authority makes the division of labor difficult. Equalities make more sense (each person does possess some human qualities) in close societies. Thus, equities are characteristically small and therefore, mobile. Since they often split, they do turn to be numerous. But they are place their equivalent turns up in another little quell and dispensed these qualities are easy to attack but hard to kill off altogether.

The very diversity of its political forms saved Nuer culture from early demise. Along it continues between the extremes there: Stronger and Weaker. Various hierarchies modify equity and equities affected by hierarchy. After all they are collectives. At any one time, consequently, there are sufficiently large numbers of dispensed and varied regime adapted to different circumstances to prevent permanent damage.

If the entire cultural milieu (complete) is made up of constant (hierarchies) it can hardly adapt to change. Strand (segments) that do reproduce (develop) diversity, however can vary to keep otters (opposition) constant. Such is a rule that political regime has played in Nuer life. No one regime but all the variants taken together have learn the shock absorbers of Nuer Religion, making up with their resilience the rigidity of religious belief and the constancy of its practice (Duany 2012).

Mobilization of Military Capabilities

Decision making authority is distributed in Nuer defense system in accordance with the many regulatory ideas or laws in the Nuer system of governance (Duany, 1992; Kelly, 1985; Douglas,1980; Evans-Pritchard,1940). Nuer institutions that distribute power widely rather than concentrating it in the hands of a few, foster collective identity and openness in the development of defensive capabilities are the soul values of the existence in life. The creation of complementary opposition and alliances prevents smaller groups from being disadvantaged.

Defensive and offensive forces are organized at the level of the household, the village, the cattle camp, the district, the regional section, and with other peoples beyond regional boundaries. In accordance with Nuer tradition, the institutions of elders, household heads, custodians, and religious leaders are expected to serve as trustees for their mobilization of military capabilities among the Nuer. Any threats against them can leads to quick mobilization for self-defense.

Method Organizing for Security and Defense

There are methods of security at many different organizational levels in Nuer society. Households in villages or in separate clusters of windscreen in cattle camps share land and water resources. If households come into conflict with each other, the members of each family must be prepared to defend themselves. Members of households or villagers or cattle camps may, upon occasion, need the assistance of others in protecting their lives and property. Kin groups or political units such as villages, however, vary in size. A small political unit increases its vulnerability to aggression by more powerful opponents.

Segmentary complementarily is one way Nuer resolve this size dilemma. When giving support is necessary, related teams or segments can aggregate sufficient forces to defend themselves against an over powering segment. Each of these segments is composed of lower-level geographically related nits that can advantages of both the large regional organization and the small independent segment. If insurrection occurs in one of the segments, other segments can be mobilized independently to stop the disturbances. If corruption arises in some part of Nuerland, remedies are usually sought through alternative segments of the society. The grounding segmentary complementarily in genealogical structures and the freedom of action of individuals provide the Nuer with the ability to combine in large numbers against external forces and to cope with internal conflict.

Although segments at different levels of organization can combine to thwart aggression, segments also fight among themselves. However, a few basic rules govern behavior within a region and also across regional boundaries. First, individuals have a right to demand compensation for injury. Second, aggressors are obliged to pay compensation in cattle. Because of the high value placed on vengeance as a principle, among the

Nuer, multiple agents with limited jurisdiction are authorized to resolve conflict and take leadership in mediating peace in the community.

All Nuer recognize the right to vengeance where compensation is not paid. The vengeance group is composed of the militia of the segment to which the injured party belongs. The size of the militia depends upon the relative positions of the aggressor and the victim within the existing lineage structure and the number of allies and friends each side can muster. Because of the great distances involved, the membership of the militia is rarely drawn from above the level of the region.

This traditional security system gives the Nuer upper hand in term of defense among South Sudanese communities. The principles and symbols of *Bunaam* currently call White Army are training to master war skills, being courageous, trust, respect and commitment to the organization. The working rules of collective action are in the heart of this institution.

Limiting Shirking

Individuals working together as a team can accomplish tasks that cannot be accomplished by individuals acting alone. Good teamwork, among the Nuer, yields stability and security for Nuer families. Preventing shirking is necessary, however, for the continued success of teamwork. If there is no accepted and enforceable means of preventing shirking, individuals will do what they want, disregarding common security and defense requirements. The quality of teamwork will eventually decline, and in turn, the welfare of the members will suffer.

Shirking in SPLM/A factions is recognized. A lack of acceptable norms to control shirking has weakened the liberation movement. The bad conditions of the refugees camps life was a big contributor to the shirking in the SPLM/A. Some junior commanders and soldiers were compelled to do the fighting and while senior commanders were permitted to live in the cities or leave camps without carrying the burden of fighting and without justifiable reason for not being in the southern Sudan with the combatants. Dinka Bor and other Dinka groups as well have been accused of shirking. This situation was resented by some ethnic groups and has led to desertion or disengagement. Unless serious measures were taken, it was likely that many more officers were able to leave the movement and settled in urban centers in East African countries.

Among the Nuer, the active participation of each member is an important source of success. It is necessary for members to monitor each other's performance to prevent shirking in order to maintain a high level of participation in teamwork. Responsibility for monitoring performance assigned to members of a household, household heads, age-set leaders, and *Buuthrem* (leaders of the fighting teams). Mutual monitoring and enforcement is possible because people fight in units composed of members of village or cattle camps. The village and the cattle camp contain the same peoples at different time of the year, which are relied upon for large scale conflict. These village or camp groups are small enough so that individuals know each other and can monitor each other's behavior. There are costs for individuals who attempts to shirk.

Cooperation is usually preferred to shirking on the basis of self-interest and the interest of one's family. If one villager does not fight, others may decide not to fight. If villagers do not defend their interests, all will loose and become subjects to the one who defeated them. It is in the best interest of all able bodies' adult males in a village to cooperate towards off external aggression. Most members of a community want their village to continue to be viable and their way of life to be maintained against disturbances. Size of a group does affect individual calculation. In a small group one individual makes a greater difference than he or she does in a large group.

Coordinating the security and defense activities of Nuer segmentary militia requires trust and experience. Elders, age-set leaders, and custodians are perceived to have the necessary experience to prepare them for the serious business of war. The basic skills learned from the training camps or earlier ages are made perfect by practice in fighting through the years. These persons are also believed to be able to guard against momentary passions and irrationalities that might place a community in unwarranted danger.

The Nuer segentary defense force is guided by building trust among the young warriors. The building of trust and caring for each other is taught through folk tales. One of the most folk tales is how to settle the dispute among age-mate as follow:

> Once upon a time two cats went fishing and caught a fish. One wanted to divide it. The other was distrustful and he said, "No, let us get someone to divide it for us. I think the chief of the monkey tribe will be our judge." The cats went to the monkey chief and asked him to be the judge. Very quickly, the monkey responded, "Yes, with my pleasure. "He took the knife. Instead of cutting the fish in halves, he made one piece larger than the other. As he raise it up and said, "I didn't divide this well." So he took a full bite out of the heavier side.

> "What are you doing?" The cats asked.

> I'm going to eat on this piece to make it even with the other. You trust me right?" The cats were not sure whether they trust the monkey anymore.

> As he ate it, it became lighter than the other piece, so he changed over and began to eat the other to even the balance.

> The cats saw that the monkey intended to eat all the fish. "Mr. Judge, let us have the balance of the fish, and we will divide it ourselves," they said.

Okay, "I hope there will be no fighting among you, then the king of the animals would come after you and that is no other than the lion."

He went on eating the fish on one side then the other side. The cats saw that nothing would be left but the bones. One cat turned to the other and said, "It would have been better for us to have divided our fish ourselves.

After the monkey had eaten it all, he said, "Let us all go in peace and never again let your interest blind your understanding and trust for one another."

This story is the basis for the trust among the Nuer segmentary defense force. They are bond by the trust and common good for all not the individual interest. When Nuer youth go to war they never let down each other. They can save each other life or die together as men defending their community. They take it as duty and service for the Nuer nation.

CHAPTER SIX

The Peace Mission and its Accomplishments

Purpose of Mission: Peace Facilitation

THE MAIN PURPOSE of our mission in August 1993 was to attempt to bring the rival liberation movement leaders together to reconcile their differences and to stop inter-factional fighting. We consulted John Garang, Bona Malual and Francis Deng but they made it clear, as they saw the situation at the time, to us that the major problem in this regard was Riek Machar and his group who did not want to talk to John Garang in order to resolve the killings of the innocent people in the southern Sudan. We thought that we could bring the two men together since we have not taken sides with any of the factions and both trusted us as persons who can facilitate peace process and can mediate between them.

The second objective of the trip was to begin to assist the South in establishing institutional arrangements that, while rooted in the past, are efforts to meet the needs of people under intense pressure. We believe that social and political cohesion for the southern Sudanese can only be achieved with more self-conscious efforts, with wise acknowledgement of the differences among ethnic groups, with institutional arrangements that promote willing adherence and community of interest that make up the southern Sudan. That is to say the South Sudan's leadership must show greater intelligence in political and social organization, and in communication. The South cannot afford inter-ethnic wars. Such conflicts set the clock back and leave the deep wounds that were created by such conflict does not wholly heal in a short time.

It was for these purposes that we traveled to Sudan via Nairobi in an attempt to bring about discussions between Dr. Riek Machar, Chairman and Commander-in-Chief of the SPLM/A-United and Dr. John Garang, Chairman and Commander-in Chief of the SPLM/A-Mainstream with the view to their reconciliation. Many people have been and were still involved in this mission of reconciliation now between Riek and Kiir. God was at the center of all that had happened including our health and safety in this initiative for peace in the Sudan. We give account of places and the people we visited.

Places and People Visited

Commander John Garang

We met John Garang on August 19, 1993 in Nairobi, Kenya. But before we met Garang, Julia and I (Wal) met Dr. Justin Yac Arop on August 16, 1993 to make arrangements for our meeting with John Garang. Dr. Justin Arop showered us with the traditional Sudanese hospitality. He arranged for us to meet Garang. The meetings with Garang were useful in the sense of understanding the problem underlying the conflict between the factions of SPLM/A. According to John Garang, the major obstacle to reconciliation and unity of SPLM/A was the fact that Riek Machar refuse to talk to him (John Garang) and to other people who sincerely wanted to reconcile the differences.

The differences between Garang and Riek were not entirely clear, but our standing was the internal conflicts, whether in the country or in the ruling SPLM/A, have not been a contest between rival ethnic groups but among leaders. Garang maintained that Riek Machar attempted to oust the leadership of SPLM/A but failed. Garang agreed that he and Marchar would have to talk in order to understand where they differ and where they agree. "Talking," Garang told us, can resolve our problems. John Garang told us anyone who could help to make Riek Machar come to Nairobi to meet him and other peace loving people will be a contribution to the peace process and the southern liberation movement. In short, Riek Machar was portrayed as the problem both in Nairobi and in Washington.

In our discussions with Garang, we asked him in what he believed and what would it take to achieve peace, reconciliation, and unity? John Garang was not clear in this, and we only predicted the idea, that became clearer later, that Garang wants to keep his position of leadership. This was clear in his statement that "the coup has failed" and Machar could just come back to the fold, but only in his former position. We asked if that point was negotiable and if he would like to talk with Riek face-to-face? Garang answer came so quick without thinking through it, his usual way of deceiving people.

We asked about Martin Majier Gai, Martin Makur and Martin Kalibri whose cases have been highlighted by Amnesty International. They had been arrested by Garang, released and then re-arrested and their where about are now unknown. Garang told us these men were in Kaya. Our meeting with Garang was on August 19,1993 and on that date reports from some officers of SPLM/A factions indicated that Kaya had been abandoned. A month later, the news was released that the three Martins were trying to escape and then they were shot and killed.

John Garang had some difficulty in explaining why there were more Dinka under detention than other southern Sudanese combined? We told him that many southern Sudanese stated that the reason more Dinka were under arrest was that non-Dinka are killed and not given any chance to live. The explanation was simple, any non-Dinka that got before Military Court Martials were condemned to death (Oduho, 1992:1-4). He denied this without further explanation.

The UNHCR has reported that children under 10 (ten) years of age have been taken from Kakuma, Kenya for combat purposes (UNHCR, January 1994). We met some of the children in Nairobi who claimed to have run away from the recruitment camps. We also inquired about the recruitment of children and why did he allow the churches who were ready to care for the children. He denied taking children into his army. He also dismissed the claim of the churches as false statement. Garang said that "the church members are confused and do not understand what it takes to run a liberation movement. They, churches are just good at prayers and I have accepted to work with them on creating more space for them to keep praying". He was right while the churches were praying he was planning on recruiting more children as he wage more wars against Khartoum and the southerners who were against his leadership.

Commander Riek Machar

We met Commander Simon Mori Didumo and Commander John Luk Joak on August 20, 1993 in Jumbo Holdings Limited in Nairobi. Didumo and Joak related to us the background of the conflict with Garang. Such a meeting and the documents they gave us on peace negotiations attempts were very helpful. They helped Wal greatly to travel to the parts of southern Sudan controlled by their SPLM/A-United. Wal met Riek Machar in Mankien, on September 15, 1993 in Western Upper Nile State (Unity State). SPLM/A-United is seeking a multi-option referendum in the southern Sudan to determine preferences on separation, federalism, and unity. The accusation by Garang that Riek and his faction are in league with the GOS was strongly denied.

The purpose of the mission was to discuss possibilities of starting talks with John Garang. Machar was willing to meet Garang and he welcomed more international involvement in such a meeting. On the basis of this willingness, we returned to Nairobi on October 5, 1993 to meet John Garang only to be told that he had left the day before we got to Nairobi. He was reported to have gone to Narus, a military camp near the Kenya border. Thus, it was not possible to speak with Garang until we all met again at the Washington Conference. The same Garang who asked us to get Riek so that they can talk, we came to believe that John Garang was not really serious in talking. After finishing our assigning of getting Riek to accept talking to Garang we began to make contact with Garang office, the process became a long waiting period. He began to avoid our contact and leveled us as supporters of Riek Machar.

Whoever among the south Sudanese that want to get involve in bringing the two men together always gets disappointed because the mission was tiresome and could end-up without bearing fruits. Garang is a very creative procrastinator and master of so many tricks, when he does not want to do something he will keep giving you appointments that he never honored. He will creates things and play delay tactics till the initiative will die somewhere with no results. Our mission to bring Garang and Riek together was a challenge that was paved with many detours. We did not give-up but took every detour that we encountered to bring Riek Machar and John Garang together.

Besides all this division among the South Sudanese groups mounted by anti-Garang there was one uniting factor the conviction and commitment to self-determination. In 2001 all groups in Khartoum came together under Paulino Matieb command as South Sudan Defense Force (SSDF). Matieb did only address all the security threats faced by the anti-Garang group. Threats existed in many forms and were not limited to armed conflict alone. There were numerous armed threats in South Sudan ranging from small bandits groups to renewed war with the North, but the people of South Sudan also face numerous others. This include political threats lead by the Sudan Government who mounted efforts with outsiders and internal forces to disrupt the unity of the South in order to practice divide and rule policies and threats to the full implementation of any agreement reach with north.

Another threat was that the south is confronted by economic, cultural/ societal and environmental issues.

New Sudan Council of Churches

We also met with Roger and Carolyn Schrock of the New Sudan Council of Churches, Bishop Nathaniel Garang of Bor Diocese, the Acting Chairman of the NSCC and Presbyterian members of the NSCC, and others on August 16, 1993.33. The purpose of these meetings was to bring us up to date on the latest developments in the war. They informed us about churches where clergy had been forbidden to preach, churches in the Upper Nile region that had been burned down, human rights abuses by all parties in the war (for example, people had been killed in their hospital beds). They reported that the SPLM/A had strayed from its objective of liberation and had turned its guns on the people. They had burned Acholi, Bari, Didiga, Lou, Gaajok, Gaajak Nuer, Murle, and Taposa villages. The church clergy were beaten and made to carry arms and other supplies for the army.

These church members are committed to helping to facilitate settlement of the Sudan problem. They want the world to respond to the needs of the southern Sudan and want to see more international involvement. However, the New Sudan Council of Churches was now as divided as the SPLM/A. Some churchmen were obviously with SPLM/A-Mainstream, and others were supporters of SPLM/A-United. Their division had undermined their effectiveness in the peace process. They were issue oriented rather than being guided by principles of peace and democracy that have a close affinity with the idea of equality before our Creator.

If the NSCC was going to regain the respect of others and increase its effectiveness in the peace process, it must increase its capabilities to communicate intelligibly with leaders of the factions and other peace facilitators. This will entail understanding the biases and prejudices of the parties to the conflict. Second, NSCC must increase its involvement with the educated southern Sudanese both in the urban centers in East Africa and in the southern Sudan. The future lies in getting involved with the people of the south, and this means the people of different ethnic groups in the three regions of southern Sudan, Bahr el Ghazal, Equatoria, and Upper Nile. It was these educated people that would effectively bring change in the conflict between the factions of the SPLM/A. To sideline the people is just like dealing with a head without the body. It was the people who define and shape their political destiny and education helps in mapping out that course. To ignore the educated South Sudanese was to undermine the very purpose of the New Sudan Council of Churches and the peace movement at the grassroots. The churches continued to call for reconciliation made Garang very uncomfortable and he lashed at the churches and calling them names as "peace vultures" and behind them is the Whiteman money.

The Political Developments 1994-2000

The political developments indicate that the international community is slowly catching up with the "forgotten tragedy" in the southern Sudan. The World Bank has closed down its operation in the Sudan. IMF has also withdrawn voting rights from the country. The UN Commission on Human Rights has publicly condemned Sudan and its Rapporteur, Dr. Gasper Biro, has conducted in-depth investigations into the position of Sudan. Amnesty International has roundly condemned Khartoum and all SPLM/A faction for human rights abuses.

Inter-governmental Authority on Drought and Decertification (IGAD) has recently formed a commission to find a solution to the Sudan problem. The member states of IGAD are: Eriteria, Ethiopia, Kenya, Somalia, Sudan, and Uganda. The commission was chaired by President Moi of Kenya. President Moi worked consistently worked to reconcile the factions of SPLM/A even before he became the chairman of IGAD's Commissions. The Washington Declaration assigned the commission responsibility for facilitation the realization of the beginning on November 4, 1993.

The most encouraging development was the "Washington Declaration." This was an agreement on the principles of peace between the rival liberation movements in southern Sudan. Dr. Riek Machar and Dr. John Garang, Commanders of opposing factions of the SPLM/A agreed on eight points. But to Garang it was a matter of time for Riek's faction to disband while he continued with recruitment of the Equatorians who will fill the vacuum that was left by the Nuer in the battle fields. What he did know was that the Equatorains were just looking for political positions to be representatives in urban areas but not as foot soldiers. The only Equatorian group who could become foot soldiers were from the Mundari people. But the Mundari group was a very strong ally of the Sudan government under Gen, Clement Wani Konga.

The vacuum which was created gave this new chance for the Equatorians to find their ways into the movement and fill in the positions left by Nuer. One evening we had a meeting with Garang trying to follow-up some of requests on our travel to the south. While were waiting in the living-room for about two hours while Garang was meeting some Equatorians who were brought by James Wani to join the movement. We could hear the laughter of group men in nearby room. When finally Garang joint us in the living room, he apologized for the delayed and related the whole story that, 'he was meeting the new comers brought to him and among them the Cartoonist who has been keeping us laughing when we are morally depress, that was not other than James Wani Igga'; we also joint in the laughter.

After ten years of civil war (1983-93), and after more than 2.5 million southern Sudanese have lost their lives, the international community was not showing signs of concern about the fate of the southern Sudanese. Despite all the condemnation there was no sign, however, that we were closer to real political initiative that would bring a lasting peace to the Sudan. Government of Sudan was reported to be preparing to attack in all fronts as soon as the roads are passable.

There were other huge problems in the way of implementing the Washington Declaration. The agenda of peace, reconciliation, unity, and democracy was far from being implemented. Garang does not like the idea of unity arrived at through democratic means. According to Garang, Machar must disband SPLM/A-United and join him, or they remain two factions. Machar with his impossibilities was not ready to such an arrangement and did not accept. Machar proposes that an acceptable electoral college be created to elect one of them as the chairman of the liberation movement. Cessation of hostilities has not been affected, partly because the factions were not ready to stop fighting and partly because there was no monitoring system on the ground to document violations of the cease-fire.

It was unlikely that the cease–fire would hold without a system to monitor the activities of the opposing liberation movements. A south-south cease-fire would be difficult, if not impossible, to monitor. No foreign troops will be allowed to enter Sudanese territory. Monitoring the activities of armed forces by unarmed civilians was difficult, risky, and dangerous. Peace facilitators, including our initiative, have suggested to IGAD a simultaneous cease-fire between the GOS and Southern factions of SPLM/A. If the Government of the Sudan accepts this idea of simultaneous cessation of hostilities, then it would be possible to mobilize foreign and local resources to monitor such cessation of hostilities between the North and the South as well as between the southern factions. This was a possibility being explored while hostilities in the South continue. During most of January 1994, there was an armed settlement between the southern factions' but the Government Dry Season Offensive had already started in Eastern Equatoria and SPLM/A was dislodged from Upper Nile but was able to keep Barh el Gazal and a small area in Equatoria, Kaya, Yei, Narus and some part of western Equatoria.

Machar Coming to Nairobi

The acceptant of Riek and his team to come to Nairobi was a break through to our mission. The people in Washington and in Nairobi believed that Riek was not interested in face to face discussions with John Garang to reconcile their differences. The mission was primarily directed to persuade Commander Riek Machar to come to Nairobi to meet President Moi and Garang. However, I (Wal) went to the field and to found Commander Riek Machar was ready to meet with John Garang in Nairobi or in another place. After hard work to bring Riek Machar to Nairobi, it was to my surprise that Garang was not ready to talk to Riek Marchar for the reasons known to him. We later learnt that John Garang wanted the conflict to continue, the longer it takes the better for his survival.

The accomplishment of our mission in this regard was therefore speeding up his coming to Nairobi and to Washington. Due to his busy schedule in establishing civil institutions in the area, he might have come at the time we came to Nairobi. We later learned that Riek was a man who takes things for granted. He had to be urged to move where he is, he will sit hours after hours listening and talking without going for nature call. Everything is so simple to him that even the most dangerous thing that can endanger his own life; he will not even move an inch. In 1995 he almost lost his life in Pagak when the SPLM/A Garang section attacked, he narrowly scape the assassination attempt.

Mission and its Accomplishments

Our Peace Mission, as already mentioned earlier in this book, was to stop killing of the innocent people of the southern Sudan by their own children. We did not have magic means to handle the parties to the conflict in the South. We went with words, ideas, and the trust in the intelligence of the southern leaders involved sparing the lives of the people they claim to liberate.

There is a Nuer saying that "the work in a large field can be accomplish by using the little means you have, digging bit by bit" with the little means we had, we kept the momentum on pushing both Machar and Garang to meet. It was like using a small hoe to work in a big field. Digging every day, little by little and by bit by bit we were able to achieve our goal. Achievement of peace in the Sudan is to be understood as incremental; not as a one shot activity. Our mission took all the resources, both human and material we can muster to reach the goal of peace. In August 1993 Garang and Riek met in Washington DC. This meeting resulted into 'The Washington Declaration' in which a consequence of our peace mission should be viewed as positive step to peace in the Sudan; the CPA became a reality because of the foundation set by The Washington Declaration. Although, there were shortcomings of CPA which provided a roadmap for South Sudanese to get their independent, but the commitment of the majority of South Sudanese landed them to the promise land.

Washington Declaration 1993

The most important achievement of peace mission was the face to face meeting of Commander Garang and Commander Machar. Without the peace mission, the Washington Agreement would have unlikely occurred in October 1993. A lot of efforts, however, were put into the realization of the meeting in Washington by many people, especially, Harry Johnson, Chairman, sub-Committee of Africa in the House Committee on Foreign Relations of the US of representatives.

Washington Declaration was an agreement between Dr. Riek Machar and Dr. John Garang for the first time in two and half years. They agreed on the following principles of peace:

a. Agreed on the right of self-determination for the people of the southern Sudan, Nuba Mountains, and marginalized areas.
b. Agreed to an immediate cessation of hostilities and monitoring of this agreement.

c. Agreed to set an agenda for peace, reconciliation, unity, and democracy.

d. Recognized that the conflict between us must be resolved through peaceful and democratic means.

e. Appreciate and encourage the regional effort for peace, reconciliation, and unity in southern Sudan, Nuba Mountains, and other marginalized areas, and call upon the international community to support this effort;

f. Agreed to cooperate and facilitate relief work in areas where people are affected by war, famine, and disease;

g. Agreed to oppose the policies of the NIF government in Khartoum, and other subsequent regimes that deny the right to self-determination of the people of southern Blue Nile, Nuba Mountains and other marginalized areas; and

h. Agreed to inform the regional leaders of this agreement, and urge that the allow-up meeting take place to no later than November 15, 1993.

The Washington Declaration was a foundational Conner-stone for peace in the Sudan. The forgotten tragedy in the Sudan was human creation and must be resolved by using human endeavors and that encouraged us to use our resources to contribute to peace process in the Sudan. Involvement of many people concern with the Sudan in the US government, particularly the southern Sudanese in diaspora was a key in bringing peace in the Sudan. Garang tried to down play the important of the Washington Declaration, but the American took interest and building on it to the end of signing of the CPA 2005.

CHAPTER SEVEN

What was Recommanded

THE SITUATION IN the southern Sudan was worsening. At that time, the GOS had already begun major offensive in the South. There were very limited options available to the south. The army of the GOS can and must be constrained by southern Sudanese themselves. The southern Sudanese must maintain military capabilities to defend themselves and their property. The southern Sudan liberation movement must be restructured to embody the values and beliefs of disparate communities in the South. In the interim period, before re-structuring of the liberation movement, the factions of the SPLM/A, however, must work with one another and cooperate with IGAD for a negotiated peace with the GOS.

Enhancing Possibilities for Negotiated Peace Settlement

The South faces serious and unprecedented danger from the current government. The sources of this danger lies in the importation of weapons of mass destruction by the government, with the financial support of Iran, and in the government's theological commitment to the destruction of non-Islamic societies in the South. The military capabilities that the Government has acquired and its intentions portend nothing less than preparations for a genocidal war in the region, a war that would also assuredly have grave consequences for Eastern and Central Africa.

During the last three years 1994–1998 the Government of Sudan has received several billion dollars' worth of arms from China and other Muslim countries. Theologically, any real peace settlement with South was seen as an intolerable affront to Islam and a betrayal of Sudan's agreement with Iran. Short of acquiescing in the destruction of different ways of life in the South, therefore, there was absolutely nothing the South can do to satisfy the Government of Sudan.

The government of Sudan wants to achieve peace on its own terms. In the talks that have been initiated in Nigeria, Nairobi, and Washington, the Government of Sudan has shown no enthusiasm for talks or for the cessation of hostilities. The Fundamentalist Government was unlikely to agree to serious negotiations while it was still in a strong military position. The North can accept the idea of a multi-option referendum only when there is enough pressure from the South. Southern Sudan and international community must provide this pressure to end the sufferings and war related deaths in the South.

The march of Iranian or Sudanese-Style fundamentalism was a major force threatening peace in Sudan, Northeast Africa, East and central Africa and other parts of the world including the Persian Gulf and the Middle Ease. The American ethnologist and orientalist Carleton Stevens Coon wrote in 1851 that Islam "has made possible the optimum survival and happiness of millions of human beings in an increasingly impoverished environment over a fourteen-hundred-year period" (Coon, 1951).34 As Iran has shown, Islamic extremism in the Sudan is the psychological defense mechanism of many displaced peasants threatened with the loss of traditions in pseudo-modern cities where their values are under attack. Beyond its stark, clearly articulated message, Islam's very militancy makes it attractive to the downtrodden. It is the one religion that is prepared to fight.

The costs of the war must be raised for the Government of Sudan; it must be made to realize that their policies in the South are not acceptable. The South must build its military capabilities to contain the spread of fundamentalism is not stifling the freedom of Islam as a religion. Many Sudanese Moslems do not agree with fundamentalism. Islamic states such as Egypt and Saudi Arabia are currently fighting fundamentalism.

Understanding the Need for a New Strategy

The SPLM/A has attained possession of adequate means of coercion and has terrorized the southern population into passive compliance. The predominant instruments of SPLM/A are coercion and corruption. It has not managed to integrate society around any positive political values. The SPLMA/A has been able to persist only as long as it successfully coerces, disintegrates, and demoralizes its social environment. Because the cooperation of the civil population is needed in order to carry out the liberation struggle, coercion has not been a successful strategy. Corruptions, in various doses, might have worked for some time, but it demoralizes both the commanders and the people. Reforms that are consistent with the power interests of the commander class are very few.

The probability that the people in the SPLM/A controlled areas will be able to organize according their indigenous ways of life was only partly dependent upon the strategies pursued by the people, and directly dependent upon the degree of control the SPLM/A is able to exercise. The probability is close to zero during the period of SPLM/A is able to exercise. The probability is close to zero during the period of SPLA terror. It is much higher when the strategy of corruption predominates. The crucial intervening variable is the ability of the society or the population involved to defend it against demoralization by the liberation movement.

The ability of groups to defend themselves, from demoralization by the SPLM/A differs from one group to the other. Some members of the

SPLM/A broke away to form another movement became known as the SPLM/A-United. The response of the people of Pibor, Pachalla, Torit, and Kapoeta districts has been to support the Sudanese armed forces to take over these towns from SPLA. It was ironic that people who were supposed to be interested in being liberated from the Government of Sudan would back northern troops in dislodging SPLA of the mainstream. What does this suggest to the leadership of SPLM/A-Mainstream and the people of the southern Sudan in that special time despair?

This would appear to be a serious vote of no confidence for SPLA. It was a rebellion against the ways SPLM/A has been carrying their affairs as we have described above. It is not that the people involved in supporting government troops were any less nationalistic than the southerners killing and torturing other southern without fair trial. The people were calling southern leaders and God-given resources to win the peace. The quest for self-government and self-respect in the southern Sudan requires that people there achieve a common understanding.

Otherwise, in Tocqueville's words, they will be "unable to discern the causes of their own wretchedness and (so) fall sacrifice to ills of which they are ignorant" (Tocqueville [1835] 1945,1:231). The southern Sudanese were challenged to use their brains better, to think harder, to plan more wisely, and pray more effectively for a peace that was held hostage by three warlords. Garang, Machar, Nyuon and Kuol.

Reclaiming of Mechanisms of Collective Decision-Making and Action

The fundamental problem at the root of the institutional crisis in the SPLM/A is the alienation of the SPLM/A factions from southern Sudanese society.33 The liberation movement was perceived by all southern Sudanese as an institution to lead them in the liberation of the South from the domination of the Moslem North. However, institutionalization of the top-down arrangements by the socialist group who established the SPLM/A has led to a permanent oppression of those persons in the area under the control of the movement, that is, most of rural southern Sudan. The Socialist leadership has not been accountable to the people for their actions. The SPLM/A leadership, for example, can detain anyone, can imprison any individual who provokes the displeasure of the leadership, or an even arrange for their execution. This is one of the reasons why the majority of intellectual Southern Sudanese felt the movement, for example what Soyink has called "internal political brain drain" from the movement (Soyinka, 1988:8). However, this was effective as long as the SPLM/A remain an integrated whole and the internal enemies were kept at bay.

The unlimited use of coercive power and corruption by some of the southern leaders in the movement has clearly and visible costs to the way of life of the people and to the liberation movement itself. The adverse effect, however, were not easy to identify. These costs relate to moral order and its relationship to autonomous standing of individuals and their capacity to associate with one another in self-organizing endeavors. The consequences of the SPLM/A's coercive rule on the way of life of various communities in southern Sudan were most directly visible in the degeneration of ethical norms and behavioral patterns upon which all social order must be founded. These are the norms and patterns connected with such values as reliability, honesty, trust and respect for human life.

The key point in the process of change, however, is the reclamation of the mechanisms of collective decision making and actions by society. This can happen only when the diverse mechanisms of collective action emerge again to serve the common good of the society. In order to achieve this, it is first necessary to reevaluate the private. In order to re-create the public, it is simultaneously necessary to re-create the private. Individuals, groups, it is simultaneously people functioning in the southern Soudan need a considerable measure of autonomy if they are to develop the critical self-consciousness to address themselves to the situation confronting them.

The SPLM/A has been uncompromisingly top-down. There is not, and never has been, popular participation in political and economic decision-making. Everything, on the contrary, is done to prevent the expression of popular interest, and to ensure acquiescence in policies which are hostile to the public interest. The loyalties and duties imposed on the volunteers in this war reflect the conviction that there is a moral order in the universe, and that man's well-being depends upon obedience to that order as men see it. The intrusion and coercions of British imperialism and Sudan functioning as a nation-state had wrecked that moral order. To restore that order is difficult. But without restoring it, there can be no peace or self-respect.

The South must accept voluntary mass participation as inevitable for the achievement of self-government and self-respect in southern Sudanese. The people must participate out of their will and understanding. Otherwise the alternative is defeat by the massive and stronger army from the Government of Sudan. The movement should gain a community's sympathy and support. It should, then, attempt to transform this support into active participation. Massive participation is necessary for the risk of life, for porter age of ammunition, for the building and running of schools and clinics, for meeting the requirements of local forms of self-government by local assemblies and elected executives in the zones controlled by the SPLLM/A, and meeting needs for moral restoration. This process has opportunity to succeed very well given the acephalous system of order among the majority peoples in the South.

.... Consider, wrote Amilcar Cabral of this process, the feature of an armed liberation struggle necessary to its success. These are the practice of democracy, of criticism and self-critics, the increasing own lives, the creation of schools and health services, training of cadres from peasant and worker background. All these features, and others, enable us to see that the armed liberation struggle is not only a product of culture; it is also a determination of culture (Cabral, 1979).

The danger now is the practice of democracy which is being obstructed by the SPLM/A in the South Sudan. The practice of self-governance could not wait until the total liberation of the South but today we have another liberation under way sending waves of disappointments by the population of our nation. It might be too late if we wait longer or the SPLM/A led good governance and rule of law may never occur. There was no guarantee that a culture of tolerant consensus, a culture able to promote a politics of self-development, is going to be possible, if it cannot happen now at the time our people are so badly in need.

PART TWO

SUDAN PEOPLE'S LIBRATION MOVEMENT/ARMY: 2005-2013

Destructive Style of Political Leadership

CHAPTER EIGHT

CPA a Lame Duck

"This peace of ours is like a sick man in hospital. You don't want to say for sure that he is coming home because as long as he is in the hospital and sick, he still might die". Pastor John Both Reath, South Sudanese pastor.

T HE 2005 IGAD-BROKERED Comprehensive Peace Agreement (CPA) that ended Sudan's second civil war (1983-2005) was negotiated between the SPLM/A, the leading southern movement and arms group, National Congress Party (NCP), the Sudan's ruling party. In the process of making CPA many political and arm opposition groups in the north and the south were excluded. During the interim period, in south many arm groups were absorbed into the SPLM/A, which never forged a joint platform to form one army. Within two years of the independence dissatisfaction increased and many blamed the leadership for failing to deliver on much needed security and basic services. The majority of citizens concluded that Kiir leadership style was destructive because he thinks only in terms of bravery, that giving positions to these armed groups will be satisfactory and they will not rebel anymore.

One of the reason given were that divisions between combatants and communities during the 1983 and 1991 split were not addressed and crisis within the SPLM/A grew uncheck throughout the CPA and the independence period. Another reason given was the approaching of elections in 2015 and some SPLM/A members shown their aspirants in the leadership created more divisions. The current crisis of 2013 spiraling out of ethnic violence were Dinka dominated the government and other opposing it gave a dangerous ethno-military nature within the SPLM/A (Crisis Group Africa Report 2013).

The Comprehensive Peace Agreement (CPA) signed in 2005, in South Sudan internal situation was marked by the stalemate of so inter-communal conflicts. The external and internal factors create division among the ruling party. The American and the European governments wanted the government of Sudan to take its hand off the referendum. The South Sudanese also play a fair game towards north to allow the referendum to take place, the only last card for their attaining their independence. The north was very careful on playing its cards so that they can stay out of becoming trouble or they become the next Iraq or Afghanistan.

The wide spread of the small arms and the modern weapons into the civil population was much more restricted during the Anya-nya war than in the SPLM/A period. This was enhanced by the SPLM/A's division and the government arming militias and other armed groups has resulted into spread of arms throughout the civil population in whole of Sudan. This led to the formation of such groups as the White Army among the Nuer, a formal cattle guards or Tit Weng or Gel Weng in Bahr el Ghazal, a mobile force employing designed to halt the raids of the Arabs from the North. This was reinforced by the SPLM/A by allowing all the civil population to have access to firearms and a part of strategy for self-defense. When the SPLM/A failed to protect the population from external aggressors and self-defense form the SPLM/A itself; for the record of the SPLA as protectors of the people has been patchy because some SPLM/A soliders were looters of properties of the local people (John Young 2007).

The signing of the Comprehensive Peace Agreement (CPA) was a win-win and provided sub-optimal solution to both parties of the conflict in the Sudan. However, the real test for sustaining peace depends primarily on how to address the aspirations of the people of Sudan. With peace and the imminent conclusion to decades of war, people see the future as bright and expectations were high for what it will bring: freedom, education, to end the hunger, better healthcare facilities, clean water and roads access to local markets, a total livelihood change to a better one.

From 2005 SPLM/A became a lame duck, not like the Anya-Nya led civil war was committed to independence and the people were in touch with the movement. The behavior of the SPLM/A leaders were unbearable to the people in the south, this was put in a few wards by Bishop Paridi Taban that "the people are the water and SPLM/A are fishes, when water dries the fish die." The people in South allege that the SPLM/A is fermenting violence and this could take the country back to war. It did not take long as the violence the people predicted did happened. In Jonglei the disarmament campaign in 2006 provide wide range insecurity in the State, in Unity State the SPLM/A and others point to the Missirirya as a critical agent of Khartoum in undermining peace. In Upper Nile State more revolts by the SAF/JIU, while politicians and the military offers suggest that Lam Akol's SPLM-DC has a military wing that was being supplied with weapons from Khartoum. In Lakes State the revenge killing over the cattle riding, in Warap State and North Bahr el Ghazal with inter-clan conflicts. In Western Equatoria SPLA went uncontrolled killing civilians creating insecurity state wide. From 2007-2013 the intercultural group conflicts heighten between the Lou Nuer and Murle group of Yayau and the elections 2010 conflict by George Athor who lost the elections brought the Jonglei security to hold and the widespread lawless (John Young 2007).

As internal crisis was looming other skirmishes and isolated conflicts, particularly in the north south boarders where the SAF and the SPLA were already in the dispute over Abyei and possession of critical oil producing areas like the Pan Pou (Heglig) and Karana. While all these security concerns were at the surface either party wants a return to war and the possibility that it could disrupt the oil production that both the governments depend on. According to John Young 2007 and Peter Nyaba 2013 who stated that, even without the CPA the right of the south to self-determination is widely accepted in the north and every few would be prepared to risk their lives to maintain the current fail unitary state. The CPA was unfolding with major problems the relationship between Khartoum and Juba would be fraught with tensions and the threat of violence for many years.

The people of South Sudan gave a deaf-hear to the Garang led SPLM/A called for a reformed united New Sudan. But Garang not only failed to make any significant progress in building a southern nation. What was the uniting factor for the disparate peoples of the south is the desire for self-determination and a separate state of south Sudan. Thus no matter the level of anger and frustration of the people of south have with the SPLM/A led government, they repeatedly affirmed their relationship with the north as a means to realize their aspirations for the overwhelmingly vote of 98.9% in the referendum in 2011.

Just within two year of the independence SPLM/A led government challenges mounted up to the real blowup civil war on December 15, 2013. The leadership of Salva Kiir had completely failed to tackling rampant tribalism, corruption and trying to build a South Sudanese identity, or acknowledging the realities of tribalism, the realities of the tribe and giving it a place in government as is the case of Ethiopia, the SPLM/A opposes tribalism while effectively encouraging it by its own pursuit of tribal based interests (John Young 2007). The people of South Sudan are aggrieved with all the failure and this widespread dissatisfaction, open resistance and the formation of powerful groups devoted to the protection of their communities, like the case of the Administration of Greater Pibor under General Yau Yau leadership.

With the wounds incurred by civil war, Kiir's dictatorship and lack of vision still unhealed politics in South Sudan remained marred by confrontation and chaos with irresponsible freedom. The limited experience of party-based politics, lack democracy, political leadership, lack of informed citizenship, lack of trust and unsound socio-political system, among other problems, combined to lead to unhealthy governance, non-productive political activities and widespread corruption, irregularities and bureaucracy are just parasites for lack of good governance and rule of law. South Sudanese went to war with the North so that they can direct and learn how to decide their own destiny. They fought the war because they wanted a better life.

Wrangles Imminent after South Sudan independence

The focus of South Sudan's conflict since it session from Sudan has been the state and this did not change with the advent of peace process that led to signing of the CPA. This section will focus on what the south fought for and how it was undermined by its own leaders. The continuation of centralize state attributed to the failure and denied the need for structural changes to the state, a process that alone could achieve the stated ends of sustainable peace and democracy. The international community fail to see that SPLM/A lack structures that implement democratic provisions properly, but of a complete lack of collective will to oversee a democratic transformations, which begs the question of whether there ever any genuine commitment (John Young, 2012).

The majority of people of South Sudan were not surprised when things were going wrong under the government lead by SPLM/A. The six years of interim government with Sudan and the two years of independence; the behavior of the leadership of the SPLM members was a disgrace to the liberation of the south. There was rampant corruption that led to lack of social services such as education, health, infrastructures, clean water, rule of law; it was a total lack of good governance, South Sudan became a police state or in a stage of becoming a failed state.

The SPLM leader, Gen. Kiir Mayardit was a tower figure, around whom the entire state building process was largely built and indeed upon which the international community policy in South Sudan was largely based. As a result, the state building process bequeathed a largely dysfunctional in the South under an authoritarian ruling party (SPLM) that was dependent upon the international community for the foreseeable future (Young, 2012). The peace that the people of South Sudan were longing for was that one defined by Bendana 2002,

> "Peace is more than cessation of military hostilities, more than simple political stability. Peace is the present of justice and peace-building entailed addressing all factors and forces that stand as impediments to the realization of all human rights for all human beings."

In 2011, the President carefully-worded statement which may have sounded more like rhetoric, but it certainly carried deeper meanings then anyone could ever imagine. The unexpected message by South Sudan President, Gen. Salva Kiir Mayardit, advising those already "warming up" for his current position after the Referendum, never to undermine the choice of the southern population was strongly echoed in his many speeches.

"If there are people who are warming up and hoping that Salva will step down after the Referendum, I want to say that they are wrong because I will not disappoint the people of Southern Sudan who voted for me overwhelmingly to lead then during this critical period in history," Kiir, also Sudan First Vice President said as he addressed 2011 opening of the second parliamentary session.

However, while others said it was still too early for him to declaration of the official referendum results, the President's close allies, already certain about the final verdict, say it was time to call the short.

The Tonj North legislator, Hon. Aleu A. Aleu, was quick to challenge the President to name those whom he accused of undermining the choice of the southern population; the voters who gave him over 90% of the votes in the 2010, April general elections.

"I heard the President saying those warming-up for his seat should respect the choice of the people. But who are these people? The President should openly declare their names before members of this August House (Parliament)," Hon. Aleu said, while reacting to the president's speech during the next day's Parliamentary session. What the people of South Sudan did know was that the cat was sharpening it claws to get ready for destruction of rat nation.

Gen. Kiir's impromptu revelations, political analysts argue, could have been provoked by an imminent power struggle likely to arise within the Sudan People's Liberation Movement (SPLM) hierarchy after independence. Senior members within the south ruling party (government), they added, are likely to emerge to challenge the incumbent for the Presidency of the Africa's youngest nation. Interestingly, Hon. Onyoti Adigo Nyikwec, the Minority Leader, National Legislative Assembly (SSLA) seems to share the same view of looming power struggle likely to crop up within the SPLM leadership.

"Well, for us in the opposition, we have no doubt in the leadership capabilities of the current leadership under President Kiir Mayardit. But there is a power vacuum and some people have already shown interest, perhaps that's within the SPLM party," Hon. Onyoti said, to a rapturous applause. That was unfortunate for Hon. Onyoti who did not read the history of SPLM/A and what the future its hold.

The other contentious issue, he said, was whether the recommendations of the historic South Sudan political parties' dialogue held in Juba 2010, and would really be implemented. This die out as the SPLM ignore it.

In one of their resolutions, the SPLM and leaders from the other nine political parties unanimously agreed to form an all-inclusive government soon after the referendum. Are we likely to see new elections of state

Governors, Commissioners and even MPs? Well, that was one of the key issues agreed upon during the dialogue.

Almost a week prior the Gen. Kiir's national address, Rtd. Gen. Joseph Lagu, his aide on general duties, openly advised the post-referendum leadership never to repeat the mistakes made by previous regimes. Such mistakes, he added, centered on widespread tribalism, nepotism unequal power distribution and accumulation of wealth (corruption at its height). Among the government ministers and generals and in all organized forces.

"Let's not follow the steps taken by the successive northern regimes. There are usually many advantages that come with power, but the problem is that those in charge are tempted to hang on for so long. One man sitting in the chair for years is an insult to the rest of the population," Rtd. Gen. Lagu told journalist at a news conference in the South Sudan capital, Juba. Lagu a military man understood the body language of Kiir.

Specifically, he emphasized, was the question of the terms limits for the presidency, which he said gives others the change to rule on the basis of democracy and good governance. "Why don't we adopt the system of terms limits used by the Americans and the British? This is the modern system of democracy widely recognized globally," the senior advisor to Kirr, flanked by Information and Broadcasting Minister, Hon. Dr. Barababa Marial Benjamin who was not ready to the statement above. Democracy is hot issue to the SPLM, whoever talk about it touch their dictatorship nerves of the leadership (Juba Monitor 2012).

So what could have triggered Gen. Kirr's early intentions for contesting the presidency of the independent South Sudan, before the actual announcement of the final referendum verdict in mid-February 2011?

A SPLM member of Parliament, who preferred anonymity, told the Parliamentarians shortly after the president's landmark speech on the

January 24ᵗʰ that Gen. Lagu's advice could have taken the president and his key political strategists by surprise, just when they thought it was still too early to make it known to the southern population.

"Joseph Lagu is an experienced politician, war veteran and an academician. His words and advice cannot be misinterpreted and taken lightly. I believe he called the short," said the SLPM legislator who refused to be quoted.

Overall, Gen. Kiir is widely seen as chosen "messiah" who having been tasked with the peoples' mandate was able to successfully guide the southern population towards a successfully peaceful, fair and transparent self-determination referendum.

The vote was a key prerequisite of the 2005 Comprehensive Peace Agreement (CPA); the accord that brokered a peace deal to end over two-decades of bloody civil war between Christians in the south and Arab-dominated Muslims in the north of the country. An estimate nearly 2.5 million people are said to have died during the war, while nearly 4 million were displaced.

President Kiir knows how to bring the people of south to dance his music; he lauded the southern population for what he said was a spirited solidarity shown during the conduct of the referendum. Even before the final results announcement, preliminary figures shown voters over-whelmingly chose separation as opposed to unity by 98.3%, and the no tolerance to corruption which does not carry any meaning to him any longer. Who should claim the credits? It is the people of South Sudan who have never lost their vision of a separate state of their own and they came out to vote.

Consequently, Gen. Kiir was quick to remind his people about the importance of patriotism, in addition to maintaining good relations with the north of the country after independence. Although he has no idea about what was patriotism to the nation, he was soiled, seedy and fragrant with hate that kept him dealing with those politicians interested in the power.

His remarked, "As southerners, we should never allow our various undivided interests to override national interests. Nations are built by people through sacrifice, patriotism and a common goal." However, as the Southern leader received a standing ovation from the members of the National Assembly, something still lingered on the back of his mind. A charismatic with diplomatic approach to resolving contentious issues, Gen. Kiir declared his willingness to protect the grazing rights of the Messeriya nomadic tribe in the south as helping hand to easy the worries of the Messeriya and to keep North out of his back.

On the conflict in Sudan's trouble Darfur region, Kiir, also Commander-in-Chief of the Sudan's People Liberated Army (SPLA), said his government will continue advocating for a peaceful resolution of the conflict, as opposed to military solutions. Whatever that option is what his counterpart, Field Marshal Omer Hassan Al-Bashir, backs is what the country's future awaits.

It did not take too long, however, what was in Kiir mind was different, he was a wolf in the sheep clothes, what the president want and meant came to surface on the December 15, 2013. He became a really wolf and could not tolerate those who were aspirants to his leadership. The President failed to see his own weakness affiliated with his leadership, endemic corruption by his ruling party members amount to 20 billion dollars, pervasive crime, lack of an effective judiciary and acceptance of the rule of law means that, despite the endorsement of the free market by the ruling SPLM lead government, there has been little investment in the country, the economy of which is dominated by brief case locally and international companies and petty traders from his own home boys in partnership with Ethiopians, Ugandans and Kenyans. South Sudan became a clan affairs, judiciary, national bank, security and political leadership control a hand full Kiir's home boys.

POLITICS OF EVIL AND SHAME

Public money is like holy water; everyone helps himself/
herself to it. Italian Proverb.

Regimes whose rule is terror ... led by men to whom
power has meant a license to corrupt, maim and murder'
(Samuel Butler 1680).

The formation of Government of National Unity (GNU) in 2005,
many Sudanese citizens had form their political opinions on Sudan
as state during the CPA both in the north in the south. The Central
government was control by the National Congress Party (NCP), and the
Government of Southern Sudan (GOSS) was control by the SPLM/A.
The system as abusive as it was, to be a safer guide than the theory.
According Marino Ajuet, an SPLA soldier who said that, "The system
was carefully designed by Dr. John Garang as means to restrain his
rivalries by use of physical and moral codes as army commanders and
politicians that can be easily manipulations." Still further to constrain
the brutes force of the people, he deem it necessary to keep them down
by hard labor in the pretext of liberation, that they shall be necessary
to obtain liberty and freedom to shade off scanty and miserable life of
the Arab domination. The system excite in those who join SPLA was
an humble adoration and submission, as to an order of superior beings.
Becoming an SPLM/A member is like hereditary and sees oneself
as superior being and others are objects and exposed their liberty to
sufferance.

Although few among the South Sudanese had gone all these lengths of
opinion, yet many had advanced some more, some less on the way to
understand what the system was all about. The SPLM/A draw a codes
of power as tight as they obtain to grantees and lessen the dependence
of the general functions of the communities on their constituencies,
to subject to those of the liberation and to weaken their means of
maintaining the steady local systems and hence dismantling the social

structure that kept these communities for hundreds of years. For South Sudan to recover, therefore, in practice the powers which the SPLM/A had built, control and to warp to their own wishes led to the downfall of the South Sudan as a nation.

The whole point of the predicament of partially is that human beings are sometimes invariably blind to an objective, detached, neutral perception of complex historical situation they found themselves in. People interpret events; see events from their own perspective. They see that perspective for what it is only when they are given a new perspective when they do not give themselves. South Sudan under Kiir have been struggling to offer way-out of many problems, however, the leadership has lost the ability to objectively assess and weigh-up all the evils it had created. The evils of torture, oppression, injustice, immorality, tribalism and corruption have become the norms that guide the SPLM/A system. This has affected the society as whole because the generations had operated with perspectives from which they doubtless are able to assess the blindness that characterize the present perspectives.

The dream of the people of South Sudan on the contrary, was to maintain the will of the majority of the convention and the people themselves. Their believed as guided by the principles of democracy, "that man was a rational animal, endowed by the nature with rights and with an innate sense of justice and that he could be restrained from wrong and protected in right, by moderate powers confined to persons of his own choice and held to their duties by dependence on his own will" (Padover 1936). The SPLM/A complicated organization control by one man was the intelligent nor best to effect the happiness of South Sudanese; that wisdom couple with evil genius trapped South Sudanese in such machinery of corruption that breed bad leadership and an expensive selfish lifestyle. The principles of transparent, accountability, rule of law and human rights are concepts unknown to SPLM/A leadership.

The majority of South Sudanese believed that after the liberation they will enjoy at ease the security and the full fruits of their own labor, enlisted by all their interests on the side of law and order, habituated to think for themselves and to follow their reasoning (constitution) as their guide. They believe that they would be more easily support the system and safely governed, not by the evils minds nourished in error, vitiated and debased as in Marxist thinking, guided with ignorance, indigence and oppression. They continued to believe that the cherishment of the people then was the democratic principles; however, the fear and distrust of their leaders override their liberation. The people of South Sudan cannot be less anxious for a government of law and order which is the strongholds of federalism; no one enjoys liberty unless s/he uses it. Their efforts to continue to such for good governance based on the constitution, human rights, rule of law will be the road to freedom, order and prosperity of their nation.

WINNERS AND LOSERS

"Our noble cause brought down by our leaders'
selfishness" (Julia Duany 2013)

During the CPA the oil money follow like the River Nile water, SPLM/A leaders did made a considerable celebration about their contributions to liberation and this created winners and losers. They kept reminding the people of South Sudan that "we liberated you". Although the public is aware about high corruption and kept critics on the right of the political spectrum that the SPLM/A is recklessly hurling public resources into their own banks accounts in the foreign countries, President Kiir for example proclaims: 'The SPLM/A members believe that they have the right to be rewarded and continued to mislead public that he is fighting corruption. He kept ensuring the public that he knows that the SPLM/A program is as helpful as possible to many South Sudanese who may be able do business and improve livelihood, so there is enough resources to do development in the country'. In 2014, the Government gave irresponsible statement in Donor Meeting, Norway that, 'South Sudan is like a young child who can break a few classes here and there and should not be punished for the mistakes s/he made'. This statement brand South Sudan with horrible image of a brad child brought up by irresponsible parents who lack guidance and order to raise the child well. They have become victims of their own votes for independence. We have hand over the key for the goats' fence to the wolves, said a one pastor in a Sunday sermon (Fr. Santo March 2015).

The challenge that is facing South Sudan as a nation, however, is the destructive style of political and economic leadership, and that the SPLM/A leaders did not really commit themselves development of the country. Because they know this and still devote their public speeches and stressing that the country is young and will take time to develop. While SPLM/A leaders could have excused themselves for being unable to run the country, they just continued with their liberation style leadership which is undemocratic and top down approach.

The CPA which last for six years was a period marked by a shaky peace and bad governance, South Sudan suffered from lack of visionary and altruistic consumer leaders who are not committed to the welfare of their own people. The independent was marked so fluttered by the new-founded power and prestige in the new state, many SPLM/A members became sucked into a mechanism which facilitates and continued exploitation of South Sudanese. It was easy for the new rulers to be blinded with material wealth and privileges associated with wealth and political power because they were naïve and inexperience in the art of governance. This development allowed the beginning of small group of illiterate South Sudanese who were members of commander class to exploit public resources while ignoring the fate of the impoverished majority. With bad beginning, leadership became characterized by opportunism, personal advancement and enriching at the expense of the masses.

The few South Sudanese leaders who demonstrated visionary leadership have been misunderstood and unsupported due to naivety and ignorance about the political forces at play in South Sudan. SPLM/A leaders were the darling of international partners and receive huge support especially in form of security aid which sustains them in power creating a one party system. These leaders consolidated their massive local militias and networks of secret service that terrorize their own citizens. So the citizens continued to live under regime where freedom of the press and information is curtailed and citizens to seek police clearance before any assembly, those without licenses, pass or permits face punishment. The December 15, 2013 ethnic cleaning in Juba was a creation of political leadership rather than regular animosity over ethnicity on grassing lands and water pools. The people of South Sudan if properly guided, they would live together peacefully as they have done for generations and would negotiate over whatever differences emerge over the resources, whether in water resources, fishing pools and grazing lands. They had done so before and they will still do through negotiations rather than inter-ethnic fighting. Our South Sudanese communities have skills and rich traditional methods of peace-making.

The threats to the communities are more political system that is being challenged by a strong civil society that forced leaders to hide and cling to their ethnic group to control economy. This system encourage and fuel the worst violent as what happen recently in South Sudan. It was not the communities who want to fight, but threaten few Politicians who fear of losing power. It became evident that Kiir trained fifteen thousand militiamen from his own ethnic Dinka to protect him from the pressure that was coming within his own SPLM/A party (Nyaba, 2013). This is a short leave for leaders who think that they can control their citizens through the power of terror, but when things get worst people can became a force that cannot be stop to proclaim their destiny, they will take their lives into their own hands fight for liberty and these dictators will become losers while the people become the winners. In 1994, Mandela address the public in which he commented that, 'the history of liberation is characterized by too much forgetting which saved the powerful and dispossessed the weak.'

DEMEBER 15, 2015 THINGS FALL APART

"If we open a quarrel between the past and present, we shall find that we have lost the future (Winston Churchill)

From the Bor rebellion that led to the establishment of SPLM/A in 1983 was not by surprise but the usual coming together of the South Sudanese, particularly the Nuer and the Dinka to stage the cause of the south. The historical records provide a strong evidence of the National movement in Sudan in 1920s with formation of the anti-British White Brigade founded by two South Sudanese, Ali Abdalatif, a Dinka and Abdalfadheel el Maz, a Nuer (Mamdani 2014).

A similar story is told of collaboration between Kurbino Kuanyin Bol, a Dinka and William Nyuon Bany, a Nuer, both former officers in Sudan army, led to the 1983 munity in Bor and Ayod. This mutiny led to the second phase of the North-South struggle (Young 2011; Mamdani 2014). But getting together among the South Sudanese sometimes does generate tragic results. From 1983 to 1991 was very bloody to South Sudanese rural communities. However, the memories of 1991 where 2,000 Bor Dinka were killed by SPLA Nair group under the leadership of Riek had narrowed into a more or less exclusive Nuer affair. This has been the sin that Riek need not to be forgiven by Dinka leaders and the Nuer as people had to pay for it and then in 2013 blood spilt was justified and supported by the majority of Dinka leaders.

According to the African Union Report, there were at least two large massacres perpetrated in Juba, including one at J2 building adjacent to the Presidential Palace and another at the Gudele Joint Operation Center, a police station. "On the December 16, 2015, 90 Nuers and 21 soldiers were gathered by soldiers and executed with only 13 soldiers escaping. It was alleged that the 90 Nuers were civilians, many of them were government civilians' servants who were running away from the fighting that had erupted all over Juba." The 21 soldiers were Nuers who were part of the President's first ring of protection and had earlier on been disarmed by a senior military officer. It was say that, "the person who ordered the killing of the civilians and disarmed soldier was Lt. Colonel Lual Maroldit who was attached to the VIP close protection unit of Tiger Battalion or Presidential Guard. In Gudele the similar operation took place, "the targeted killing of 134 Nuer men on December 16, 2015."(African Union Report 2014).

The polarization of ethnicity inevitable led to a fragmentation of South Sudan along the ethnic lines. In one local authority after another, those claiming to be indigenous to the land fought those who they said lacked customary rights to natural resources and who in turn, demanded their own ethnic homeland. Just a few years after the independence, South Sudanese became IDPs in their own home country and seeking protection from the United Nations forces.

Did Kiir keep his words of never to take his people to war again? Not really, he turned out to be a man who never remembered what he said in one occasion to another. Kiir says one thing and does another thing. Challenged by inter-communities conflicts, he ordered the army to disarm the local communities. In 2006, about 600 Lou Nuer were massacred and over 2,000 head of cattle were looted by the SPLA (army), Wau incident where 20 people were massacres by the army, the 3,000 Murles killed, in 2011 - 2012; he ordered the army to attack the oil fields in Heilich (Panthou) in which so many lives were lost. Also, the violent conflict and armed combat that erupted in our capital on the 15th of December 2013, and since then has spread to a number of states is of deep concern to the people of South Sudan in general and particularly the Upper Nile region has been hard hit. This war has created a cycle of killings in this region which pitted one group to another. This killing of one ethnic group by another has become a norm of the day. The statistics are choking, thousands have been killed and an estimated 2.5 million driven from their homes while 1.4 Million people have crossed into neighboring countries Ethiopia, Kenya, Kenya, Sudan and Uganda. The ugliest history of South Sudan is the over 800,000 IDPs who seeking shelters in the UMISS camps around the country; citizens running away from their own government to be protected by United Nation Mission and over 2/3 of the population in brink of starvation.

The government increasingly becomes divisive, sectarian, monolithic and intolerant, unpredictable, contradicting statements and policies which the president does not deliver or practice. The priority of the government has become the corruption and bad leadership which is sustained in power mainly by deceptions, corruption and abuse of office and verbal and practical acrobatics in constitutionalism and governance and top by the loss of moral values. Leaders became canny, womanizing, liars by castigated the coup which had spread violence in the country.

The people of South Sudan had survived the previous Northern Sudanese wars and for the last eight years had learnt to live together. So, it would be sad if one's victory leads to other's demise. By turning against each other we are betraying the memory and legacy of our martyrs who died for our freedom and independence as well denying the people of South Sudan the fruits of their collective victory. The free, prosperous, peaceful, well informed and secure South Sudan, we want is evaporating like the morning mist before the harsh severe sun in the Savanna.

Civilians displaced by brutal fighting are ignoring calls from the government officials, even the President Kiir himself tries to call the IDPs to return homes, preferring the safety of squalid UN bases to risk that conflict could again engulf towns already devastated in the ongoing conflict. Citizens who saw their love ones killed and their properties looted and homes destroyed or taken over by an arm solider cannot trust again.

Many of the citizens abandoned their homes after a power struggle with the ruling party, Sudan People Liberation Movement/Army (SPLM/A) boiled over into vicious fighting that began in Juba in December 2013 and swept across the north and east of the country.

The conflict has split the army and pitted loyalists of the President Kiir against supporters of his former deputy, Riek Machar and Taban Deng Gai, a business who will clone anything to get what he want. Government troops as well as opposition fighters have been accused of massacring civilians on the basis of their ethnicity. Kiir is a Dinka while Riek is a Nuer. The coup that was later denied by the senior SPLM elites, like Edward Lino and Prof. Peter Adwok Nyaba, however, have presented strong arguments against Kiir arguments, saying that the president was not elected and has gone beyond his legitimate mandate. Let him and his supporters know that they were not given mandate to kill over 20 thousand and displacing millions of South Sudanese. They stated that "after what happened, the president must be told that he has gone far beyond his mandate, since he was not elected or mandated to lead the nation into his own home-grown-war. Let us note that, Kiir was elected to lead South Sudan to the referendum in 2010, then subsequently not mandated to lead the nation after independent in 2011 and was not elected." It was a red-line for Kiir to use his mandate to kill incident people, particularly the Nuer (Nyaba 2013).

I (Julia) visited the two UMISS camps in Juba on the February 7, 2014, what I (Julia) saw was the human catastrophe and the government blind with power keep denying the devastation they have done to their own citizens. The South Sudanese communities' lives had been ruin, lost all properties and human lives; the conditions of the camps are unbearable for human living conditions. The whole of 2014, what was working was the propaganda machine of the government, dehumanizing the IDPs. The government did not care about the lives of the people but continued to blame it on Riek and the leader of the rebellion. "Let them suffer it is all Riek's folds he started the war", said the Minister of Information. The Nuer people were taught a lesson and this is not 1991 according to the information Minister. Below are the concerns of the IDPs:

1. **Security**

   There was a great fear among the IDPs that some of their members have been disappearing. These people who left camp in search for food or those who are sick and who went to the hospital never came back. There are also many incidences of gender base violence; women who went out of the camps to find food for their families are rape by the organized forces.

2. **Camps conditions:** majority of the people are in camp because they were ethnically targeted. Anyone man who bears the Nuer cultural markings on his forehead stands a very little chance of surviving.

   a. **Health/ Sanitations:** conditions are very bad among all the people, particularly, women, children, elderly and people with special needs. The numbers of people dying, particularly children and elderly are increasing every day in large numbers. From December to February we lost over 120 people due to poor health conditions in both camps in Juba alone, Malakal, Bentieu and Bor are the worst.

   b. **Food:** there are people who go without food for days due to lack of food.

   c. **Shelters:** people are barely sleeping outside; most of shelters are made out of plastic materials which are very hot during the day and at night could not prevent the mosquitos.

   d. **Education:** many children are missing out of school and they will miss out the whole academic year; over 1,500 University of Juba students are also missing lectures. The national two universities, Upper Nile and Dr. John Garang are not functioning because the campuses are destroyed.

3. **Feeling of abandonment:** people have lost trust, because they feel that they have been abounded by their leaders and the government. One of the duties of the government is the protection of the citizens which is not forthcoming.

4. **Continue of abusive language:** the people in the camps are portrayed as the supporters of the opposition which is not the case. Many of them became victims of unknown circumstances. The government leaders continue to wage media war on the IDPs through rallies and making speeches which are divisive to

the people of South Sudan. Kiir in his speech said that the IDPs are rebels and in another speech he also said these people (IDPs) are looking for good life, even myself if I have no food I can go to UNMISS camp. (President's speeches, Nyakuren Culture Center and Freedom Hall, addressing the SPLM Youth League early February 2014, SPLM Youth League Chairman speech, Vice President Hon. Wani Igga and Mr. Akol Paul Kordit on the same occasion).

5. **State Killing of civilians:** we do ask many questions, why are the Nuers the only one ethnic group being targeted by the government soldiers when those who call for the SPLM Press Conference on December 6ᵗʰ, 2013 came from all the regions of South Sudan, among them there other ethnic groups, there Dinka, Shulik, Latuka and Zende, why Nuer in particular?

6. **Targeting of the business communities and looting of the properties:** the business communities are made-up of different nationalities from Ethiopia, Eretria, Somalia, Sudan, Uganda, Kenya and the South Sudanese as well. They are being targeted at night by the unknown gunmen, they are killed and their properties looted and not a single case has been brought to books.

The IDPs went ahead to propose some solutions to the own problems as follows:

- Restoring the respect of the sanctity of human life. The government to take the full responsibility in addressing the security issue. The security operation has gone underground and it is only our government who could identify and address the new threats. Allowing humanitarian assistance and access to all affected communities. The government institutions to reach out to their civil servants who have taken refuge in the UN camps and other countries. There is a need to address their resettlement and they should not be seen as they had abandoned their jobs. There is a great need to address their concerns, especially those who had lost properties. Identifying measures to overcome current crisis. Preaching the language of hate is not helpful in building trust of the citizens. There is a need to take reconciliation as the only approach to building trust of the people. Peace can only come when the parties to the conflict are to refrain from the negative language. Majority of our Nuer leaders are also victims like us and could not express themselves to address our conditions. Promoting peace, healing and reconciliation. A true reconciliation can be reach if different groups, women, youth, church leaders and the MPs from other South Sudanese communities, e.g. elders to reach out to the people in the camps in order to build the trust. It has been now three months and no concern from our government to find solution to our conditions in the camps. Relocation of the IDPs to places of origins: If there is no solution to the IDPs situation in the POC camps, we seek the good will of the UNMISS in South Sudan to relocate us to our places of origin. The wet season is coming and it will be better for us to be relocated to our places of origin so that we can prepare our fields for cultivations. The camps population are too large and cannot depend on UNMISS support forever. The relocation can also address the issue of education for our children and can improve health conditions at large. The leaders on both sides should take a high moral ground, particularly the government. This is a history in the making and humanity will not forgive all of us who are in the leadership positions of this beloved country. The first and most urgent matter is to secure a cessation of hostilities and a credible, verifiable process to prevent renewed violence. Some discussions and agreements had already taken place, the peace talks mediated by the Intergovernmental Authority (IGAD) but more is obviously needed since the fighting continues at this time. The urgency of sustainable peace should not distract South Sudan's people and their international supporters from the underlying, structural nature of the problem, whose solution will require not only the political solution but the neutrality of military.

A cessation of hostilities agreement signed on 23 January 2014, a recommitment to this signed on 5 May and a 9 May "agreements to resolve the crisis" were all violated within days of being signed. The Monitoring and Verification Mechanism (MVM) provided for in the 23 January agreement did not begin work until mid-April, and since then, no public information has been released about its activities. An IGAD force to protect civilians and support for MVM, but there is no indication of when the force should actually be deployed. The issue is how long are the IDPs going to be in UMMISS sites?

The UNMISS sites are full of narrative stories that bristled all with incredible adventures, so many narratives that were so reeking with bloodshed and so narrowed with hair-breadth escapes and the most engaging and unconscious soldiers with villainies. The IDPs remain speechless, wondering, shivering and worshipping when will this war end. An old man commented that, 'it is heart breaking to have a president who does not have feeling about his people. We voted for him to hold this position and he is taking it as Dinka affairs.'

Kiir Ignores International Community

There were terrible roamers going around in South Sudan, and worst of it is that half of them are ture. The United States has warned South Sudan, ready to impose sanctions on the South Sudanese leaders as Kiir snubbed talks in New York on the eleven-month conflict wracking his country. Instead Kiir sent his Foreign Minister to join the discussion on the sideline of the UN General Assembly. As his Information Minister makes provocative statements his Foreign minister tries to amend relationships with the international community.

A senior state department official told the media that, "There was a lot of disappointment expressed in the meeting that Kiir, who was in New

York, did not attend the meeting. Several of the attendees made a point of noting that Kiir was not there," the official added.

The official stressed that the east African regional block, IGAD, which been mediating sputtering peace talks, shared the view that more sanctions may be necessary. March and Kiir have been signing deals but could not break through while the IDPs are lingering in the camps not knowing when they will go to their homes.

Ban Ki-moon, the Secretary-General of the United Nations, told a high-level diplomatic meeting in New York in September 2014 that South Sudan is 'failing.' He went to said, "It has fertile land and valuable reserves of oil and it has potential vibrant economy, but instead of thriving, the country is failing."

All fingers are pointing to South Sudan leaders, and being urged to reach peace agreement and get the people out of miseries. Ban Ki–moon said, "the International Community must remain committed to impose punitive measures on those responsible for the violence and impeding the peace process." He further said, "the leaders of South Sudan are responsible for having opened the wounds that have caused so much suffering and those responsible for atrocities must face justice through mechanism that meet international standards."

He also made it clear that he opposes a declaration of amnesty for anyone responsible for killing innocent civilians, as called for the government. His speech carries very strong words to Kiir and Machar and their political rival that "they opened the wounds that caused so much suffering. Now heal them." He added that there can be no military solution to the conflict and those who impede peace negotiations or commit atrocities will ultimately have to face consequences.

This was loudly said by Archbishop Paulino Lukudu of the Catholic Church, "the current war is evil and there is no justification for killing civilians. Our population is traumatized and had been re-traumatized by the atrocities have rarely seen before. We declare this war immoral and we demand an immediate end to all the hostilities for these humanitarian concerns be addressed" he said.

The South Sudan had seen a large scale ethnic killing has created a cycle of fear, hatred and revenge. South Sudan politics is becoming ethnic, even within our churches; elements of tribalism are creeping in and creating suspicion, hindering our efforts to work for peace and reconciliation. The Archbishop went to condemn tribalism, corruption and nepotism as these elements hindered our becoming one people. He also challenge all political leaders and remind them that leadership is about services to all citizens of country, not about personal power and wealth nor favoring one community over the others.

Bishop Paridi Taban spoke on the same line of violence, he called on the government and the opposition to let go of violence, "this killing must stop, when we were fighting Sudan government their hands were full of blood, now look whose hands are full of blood, our own government, this is a shame to all of us." He went on to advice the parties to seek peace and negotiate in good faith. All these churchmen were trying to follow 1994 Mandela foot step who in 1991, he told the annual conference of the South African Methodist Church: 'We have to forgive the past but, at the same time, ensure that the dignity of the victims is restored and their plight properly addressed.' The only instrument to address this goal should be the establishment of the Truth and Reconciliation institution.

Uganda/SPLM/A Links

SPLM/A and Uganda has deepest links, a long decades of joint military cooperation. John Garang and Yoweri Museveni were colleagues who attended the school in Tanzania in the 1960s and also being the students of Walter Rodney a well-known Pan Africanist. The belief was that Uganda and South Sudan relationships linked was since the time of Idi Amin's rule in 1971-1979. Amin army was made up of the majority of South Sudanese from Equatoria, particularly the Madi, Kuku, Kakuwa and other Bari speaking groups. During the SPLM/A war in the 1980s-1990s the Uganda forces were deployed beside the SPLM/A forces to counter the Lord's Resistance Army (LRA) on the pretext that the Sudan government was supporting the LRA.

When conflict broke out in December 15, 2013, the Uganda forces moved in Juba, including an air wing secured the capturing of Juba from Bor by the opposition forces. Uganda's military intervention was believes it was approved by the United States Government (Crisis Group 2014). This was confirmed by the Ugandan Deputy Speaker of the National Parliament Hon. Jacob Olanya that the United States supported Uganda's actions in securing the airport and protecting Juba and in the recapture of Bor Town from the rebels. Uganda intervention in South Sudan has been criticized for its alleged economic motivation and its treatment of civilians. Uganda went as far as use of Cluster Munitions but reportedly refuses to cooperate with the investigation into use of the cluster munitions in South Sudan and denied their use (Human Right Watch 2014; Juba Post, 2012: Vol. 6).

The deployment of Uganda force in South Sudan did not go well with many South Sudanese and the African eastern regional block. This had hindered the Uganda to play an adequate role in the IGAD mediation in Addis Ababa. In June 2014 various independent and social media groups widely discussed a leaked internal memo from president's office in which president Kiir reacted to the statement by president Museveni who admitted the there was no coup attempt in Juba as alleged by the government. However, the rush from Ugandan army was really interest for South Sudan resources.

Museveni who is president Kiir's closest ally since the death of Garang and ally in the war told the heads of state at the IGAD summit during a hot closed-door debate with the rebel leader Riek Machar that the conflict was simply ignited by a misunderstanding within the units of the president guards and not a coup. Machar and other senior members of SPLM have been seeking reforms within the party, however, that alone can lead someone to death row under Kiir.

President Kiir went out to defend himself by giving statement that "President Museveni is the only leader who defended my government. He is a true friend to me and my government. The president of Uganda acted in the IGAD meeting without consulting me." Kiir reportedly said in the memo, adding that the urgent meeting needed to be held between him and Museveni in order to clear the government about what transpired in Addis Ababa. He warn his ministers not to talk against Museveni in the media and that he already spoke with the Museveni and assure him not to get worried about his no coup remarks at IGAD summit.

The media did not rest the case but keep the light on it; however the officials from the presidency quickly dismissed the reports as false that the presidency never circulates any memo. The news about Museveni u-turn on the narrative about the alleged coup was revealed by Machar. This confession led to Machar congratulate Museveni during a hot debate involving president Kiir in the presence of the IGAD heads of state when the Uganda head of state for the first time admitted there was no coup attempt in Juba. This meeting as one of the breakthrough on story of coup attempt which Juba tried to sell to international community. Machar did not let go but also revealed that Kiir had to keep silent and could not react to his friend Museveni's position during the debate. The really story came out that the December 15, 2013 crisis was fabricated by Kiir and Museveni in order to get rid of rival political reformist within the ruling SPLM party, resulting to the imposed war on Machar's resistance movement. The confession by Musvseni was truthfully embarrassing to president Kiir. An observer at the Addis Ababa peace talks between the two warring parties said, "The remarks were an embarrassing to Kiir who only depended on president Museveni to help him sell the coup attempt narrative as other regional governments and the international community has from the onset rejected the allegation".

It is not the first time that the Ugandan leader altered statements that were seen by many to have embarrassed his South Sudan counterpart. It was just after few months while speaking at a political party gathering in support of one of his party candidates in Uganda, president Museveni said he would "hang himself" if his country was to depend on foreign troops like South Sudan. Kiir tried to ignore Museveni bad mouth, but the statements attracted fierce criticisms from the Kiir supporters with some calling for Ugandan leader to retract the remarks and apologies to the government and people of South Sudan.

Machar had voiced concerns about Museveni role, saying he has damaging political influence on South Sudan, this entire crisis faced by his country is because Kiir's decisions are architecting by Museveni who is selling his military might both providing thousand ground troops and actively air force against Machar's forces who are made-up civilians fighting because their relatives were killed. In 2014, it became clear that the Minister of Defense, Kuol Manyang did made an agreement to pay the bill for Uganda forces which amount to millions of dollars. Each soldier was paid 3,000 USD a month and compensations for those who lost their lives.

Kiir becoming abscess with Machar's continues of demand for reforms reminded us of the real drama that happened during the Africa Head of States Summit in Kampala (Uganda) in 1976. This story was related by the former OAU Information Secretary, Ibrahim Dagash 2006, as follow: "President Idi Amin was in command, chairing the session, when his aides presented him with a note. He announced from the podium: "My dear bothers and colleagues, I need to inform you that one of us has lost his seat," The dramatic announcement turned the conference hall into a turmoil, as each Head of State blood pressure short-up and thought he was the one concerned, notably General Nimiery of Sudan who turned to his entourage and loudly said in Arabic: "Did the stupid bastards make it?" Amin took his time and eventually intervened to say that a coup had taken place in Nigeria. Nigeria Head of State, General

Yakub Gowon, solemnly stood up, put his cap on his head and left the conference hall."

Because of fear of losing power, President Kiir had become paranoid with Riek Machar and his team of reformers that he never give any speech without mention his name, Riek did this, done that, all is his fold. Riek killed the Dinka in 1991 and he must pay for all what he had done. There has been no objective way of looking the crisis of the December 15, 2013, all the those who died deserve their death because Riek Machar stage the coup. Kiir keep addressing public in three languages, English, Arabic and Dinka, "Riek stage the coup", "*Riek amulu iglab*", and "*Riek aa wic bi akuma be doom riel*". The President's speeches will start with "*in nu Riek*" and finishes with "*in nu Riek*", an Arabic word of "it is Riek, it is Riek". What was it to the people of South Sudan that his language was mix, English-Dinka-Arabic, constructed worse, and his profanity so void of art that was an element of hate and weakness rather than strength in his conversation to address core issues. The majority of people were interviewed stated that it was Kiir who staged the coup (Nyaba 2013).

Impressions and the image of South Sudan had deteriorated badly worldwide. Two days in any other African country is far from enough time to make judgments, but 48 hours in South Sudan does leave impressions and images which portrayed SPLA soldiers as mindless robots who would not even think unless they were told to do so. Another most disturbing is the impression that IDPs in UNMISS protections sites, are many stories of rapes, killings, the brutality and deliberate backwardness of life in South Sudan become a reality. These IDPs camps are not far from resembling the 1940s Nazi concentration camps. But when it comes to the government authorities not a fact is presented; however, contradict any statements that come out of their mouths. Kiir government kept repeating their lies till the public came to believe it that Riek really made a coup and the Nuer should suffer.

The dirty little secret with the African leaders since 1960s up today is wide spread use of illegitimate surrogate wars and the African Union continues to ignore these brutal wars that are so devastating to life of millions of the African people (Cohen 2015). The South Sudan experience is not different from these experiences, the challenge of leadership that the liberators are as good leaders did not necessarily make best person to lead the government of independent nations. Kiir was an accidental president who took over from a highly talented and well-educated Dr. Garang, the hero among the heroes of the liberation movement was a miss-match choice of leadership for South Sudan. Kiir has become an ethnic prisoner because of fear of losing power; he is more concern with security of his power as his priority. He took nationhood as a power and kept his own members of Dinka tribe on the top making it difficult for him to tap into the talents of other groups, especially among the women group, he goes for those who lack the capacity, self-confidence and like the comfortable attractions of the international scene. Dealing with external issues was always easier and more comfortable than intractable with internal issues. It is also a feel-good for these women to have those nice titles than coping with rural poverty which have devastated the lives of South Sudanese rural communities.

CHAPTER NINE

CAVENANT and POLITY in SOUTH SUDAN

New order in South Sudan

THE SAD STORY of corruptions in South Sudan of how over 20 billion US dollars were looted by a hand full of individuals from the SPLM party, the conversation made one of the remembers; whom we discuss the issue of what has gone wrong with the party came out very clearly. His answer was simple and straight, "God made man, Man made money, money made man mad". One can really agree easily with this young man statement and search for answers to this grave situation in South Sudan let us to the following chapter. In another event the Deputy Minister of Foreign Affairs from Equatoria also express his disappointment in a similar manner that, "the Dinka has been looting this country at will, so let them then fight it out with the Nuers, we Equatoians will not join the war." It was not too long before the war has reached the doors of the greater Equatoians.

To understand how South Sudan communities organize themselves, it is important to see how their regulatory ideas marshal activities of the governance in acephalous, or centralize systems. We proceed by unraveling the context in which regulatory or governing ideas emerge, become liked to, and then bring together or order effective human action. Activities themselves usually imply efforts to accomplish something-to achieve results. Activities use regulatory ideas in a context where present means are being order to achieve some future good. Thus, there are circumstances where the South Sudanese different groups have developed and used regulatory ideas to marshal activates and in so doing constitute a system of order that become a way of life.

We are concern, in this chapter with political used of the ideas of covenant in South Sudan, the tradition that has adhered to that idea, the political arrangements that flow it, and the strategies for preservation of its distinct institutions and culture. Some brief discussion using the African philosophy of reconciliation and restorative justice will be explore as way to address the conflict that destroyed the fabric of South Sudanese people.

Environmental contest

In traditional societies of the South Sudan the environmental context exerts a formidable influence on the formation of culture patents, the means by which the people have developed a life style that can be sustained, and the system of governance that have been developed to enable the people to function as a community in relationship to the particular environment.3 As we have seen among the South Sudanese conflicts, the management of life cycles around the rainy and dry seasons, the raising of cattle, the role of agriculture, and the placement of streams, rivers and grazing lands and locations of fishing ponds during certain seasons of the year all have critical impact on issues of harmony. When the system of governance that has been formed over many generations, includes patterns of administration of common pool resources rather than private ownership of scare resources, issues of mediating peace and sustaining patterns of communication and cooperation in the midst of environmental pressures become more evident.

Therefore, a key contextual principle is that the environmental context of a particular people must be understood and the way that environment has shaped the people and their patterns of living must be incorporated in the analysis of the cultural heritage of the South Sudan.

Cultural Context

The ideas to which individuals have recourse, the language they used to express their ideas and to communicate issues, and the ways they marshal activities are the fundamental foundation upon which their continuing existence is built. The ideas that people use to understand their world, themselves and others create a framework of beliefs. Worldviews of the people articulate their values and formulate their commitments. Signs and rituals, life stages and age groupings, decision-making styles and systems of governance are all integrated into cultural patterns. It is only within the cultural context that one can discover who has moral authority, how leaders are chosen and removed, how law is created, interpreted, enforced and reformed. Each community has developed different styles of handing conflicts, dealing with lawbreakers and sharing power.

Global Contextual

It would be quite rare today to find a traditional society that has been untouched by the outside world. Systems of governance have been affected by colonial rule, centralized governments and militarization whether from the central government or the structure of the guerrilla movements. Traditional religious beliefs have been affected by the introduction of religious that have missionary designs and universal messages. For South Sudan traditional beliefs and systems have overlays of British and Egyptian Colonial rule, centralized governments with Arabic and Islamic orientations, rebel military movements that were engaged in fighting the central government and in conflict with other rebel factions, and six or more decades of Christian missionary influence follow by three decades of rapid church expansion under indigenous leadership. In a culture with a long history of isolation, there were sons and daughters of the people who had traveled to other countries and gained extensive academic training. The tradition has to wrestle with the modern and post-modern, handling the conflict of cultural change while also seeking to draw from indigenous resources.

Covenant as a Political Concept

Very few educated individuals seriously immersed in the trade religious and Christian's traditions have escaped the theological impact of the covenant idea. Covenant has been perceived as a whole theological concept, but on other hand, less a theological concept than a Theo-political one (....). The word itself is so frequently defined in the English language that it has become a mere common place term, if not quite freedom and democracy, then certainly the republic and constitution. Even so far too little has been written about covenant as a factor in political affairs in Africa.

Politically, a covenant involves a coming together, congregation of basically equal humans who constant with one another through morally binding pact supported or witness by God (a transcendent power), establishing with the partners a new frame work or setting on the road to a new task that can only be dissolved by mutual agreement of all the parties to it (Elazar 1995; Duany, Wal 2005).

The covenants are grounded on religious beliefs, and the foundation covenants of South Sudan ways of life. They necessarily have to do with God. They have their beginnings in the need to establish clear and binding relationships between God and humans, and among human relationships that must be understood as being political more than theological in character designed to establish lines of authority, distributions of power, political bodies and systems of law. I remember one time a priest reminded his congregation in the church in South Sudan that they respect the law because Moses was the first minister of law and justice.

Law is conceived and implemented in circumstances that define as well as necessitate its authority. Transcending the influence of immediate circumstances, enduring practices and prior events place law on a historical path that shapes the law making, and law enforcements practices. History of a people, belief, culture and circumstance determine the meaning and effectiveness of particular law and ultimately society's evolving governing framework.

Covenant and Purpose of Polities

In more secular terms, the task of politics is not only to construct civil societies compatible with human nature but to help people make the most of their potential by creating conditions and opportunities for leading the best possible lives. As Aristotle observed; people formed political associations not only to maintain life but to achieve the good life.

Politics has two faces: one is the face of power, and the other is the face of justice. Politics, as the pursuit of power and organization, is concerned (in the word of Harld Lasswell) "who gets what, when and how." However, politics is equally a matter of Justice, or the determination of who should get what, when, how and why?. Power is the means by which people organize themselves and shape their environment in order to live. Justice offers the guidelines for using power in order to live well.

Politics cannot be understood without both faces. Without understand a polity's conception of justice, or who should have power, one cannot understand clearly why certain people or groups get certain rewards, at a certain times, in certain ways. On the other hands one cannot focus properly on the pursuit of justice without also understanding the realities of the distribution of power. Both elements are present in all political questions, mutually influencing each other.

The need to pursue justice through a politics set on right path is as real in a secular age as in a religious one. The true essence of real politic is the understanding that just as politics cannot avoid the realities of human relationships and power, it cannot be detached from the pursuit of justice and the path of morality either.

The collapse of a shared moral understanding inevitably leads to a collapse of the rules of the game. We are witness to just such a collapse in many politics of our time, for precisely that reason, a collapse which has brought with it the present crisis in most African countries, particularly in South Sudan. It is the discovery of the proper moral base or foundation, and its pursuit in such a way that recognizes the realities of power that is essential for good politics. That is what the conceptual system rooted in covenant is all about. The rules of the game may emerged originally through evolutionary processes to be accepted by those bound by them as a matter of course. Once disrupted, however, they can only be restored by consent, that is to say, through covenanting. Thought covenant, the two faces of politics, power and justice are linked to become effective both morally and operationally.

Covenant and Autonomy

Cultures, systems of governance and the different peoples of the South Sudan informed by the covenantal perspective, they committed to a way of thinking and conduct that enable them to live free. They were bound together in appropriate relationships and to preserve their own integrities while sharing in a common whole; and to pursue both the necessities of human existence such as common pool resources and the same things of moral response in some reasonable balance. There is a dialectic tension between each of these dualities, which adds the requisite dynamic dimension to covenant based societies and that makes such societies covenant-informed as well as covenant-based. This dialectic tension is an integral element in covenantal systems, one which provides such systems with the necessary self-corrective mechanisms to keep them in reasonable balance over the long haul, at least so long as covenantal principles to inform the politics concerned.

Self-government was integral part of covenantal expressions of religious faith and these expressions bound a religious interpretation of free will to conscious choice in political assent. Traditional South Sudanese "harmonized earth with havens" through practical applications of faith in daily life their autonomous polices were based on a matrix for religious association, civil and personal covenants.

Thus, politics whose origins are covenantal reflect the exercise of constitutional choice and broad-base participation in constitutional design. Politics founded by covenant are essentially federal in structure or not.

The covenantal principles guiding the South Sudan institutional development provided a shared basis for interethnic confederation or common-wealth. In this way, federal principles bequeathed the rational and practical means for uniting different ethnic groups and politics for common purposes without negating established boundaries or their exiting forms of moral and political authority. Deliberative processes had to be designed to make inevitable conflicts of a diverse people and productive sounds of innovation.

Institutional capital provides the basis of shared understanding. Where it exists at the community level enables people to resolve problems. Institutional capital denotes the set of rules that members of a community share in common such as de-facto village governments, township councils, customary land tenure systems and organizations as cooperatives. Community member use these rules to channel their behavior, monitor conduct, resolve conflicts.

Understanding what institutions contribute to the strength of shared understandings. In his, Democracy in America, Alexis de Tocqueville enumerated the institutions that maintained self-government. Religion topped his list immediately followed by family. The lessons learned in families like the guidance of religion teachings, encouraged voluntarism and enhanced public life. Among the South Sudanese, family taught self-control and reciprocal regard as basic to self-governance. Established family law is also part of wider political order and contributes to the strength of understanding among the people of involved. Marriage covenants joined disparate individuals and their associations to promote broad accord or crosscutting alliance, preventing persistent differences from destroying commitments to the long-term arrangements necessary for productive undertakings.

Strategies for the Preservation of Distinct Institutions and Cultures

The state constitutions that we have surveyed showed a remarkable degree of similarity in the South Sudan even if differences persisted among regional cultures. The three region of Bahr el Gazal, Equatoria and Upper Nile differed in their public philosophy, view of liberty and orientation to political order. With the regions different periods of settlements, languages and religion or beliefs resulted institutional variations. The South Sudan if taken as a one region like other region in east Africa shared common experience on internal political crises that led to a more definitive articulation of culture and politics in increasingly explicit institutional decision-making.

In all the Sudanese regions, these internal adjustments, often maintained the distinctiveness of social life in what amounted to associational forms of confederacy. Similarly, the distinct biophysical, culture and political environments also influenced and sharped the political institutions. Part of this environment included the frame work set by the British colonial system (Duany, Wal 2006). These differences need to be taken into serious account when putting together an acceptable constitution in order to preserve distinct institutions and cultures in South Sudan.

Integration based on shared understanding for covenantal and federal principles can preserve the internal diversity of a whole system formed by the willing consent of parties who retain their capacities for constitutional and collective choice. In the Interim Constitution of

South Sudan which embedded the bill of rights that defined national, regional and state institutions were clear expressions of a federal system that's compatible with the institutional arrangements of the greatest majority of South Sudanese where the covenantal theology remained authoritative.

Processes of constitutional choice rely upon a deep understanding of how existing patterns came about and how they are relevant to changing circumstances. New orders emerge from or constructed from older orders. Knowledge and sensitivity to contemporary values, rituals and other practices that constitute the uniqueness of society are essential for successful processes of transformation. Thus, meeting the challenges of constitutional choices requires considerable pooling of knowledge and critical analysis among people themselves in discourses about their collective dilemmas, aspirations and goals; their conflicts and potential conflicts and their capacity to transform them (Amos Sawyer 2005).

The only hope for South Sudan is the emerge of the new voices, a leader who will dedicate his/her life tackling poverty, inequality and fostering tribal reconciliation to address challenges of rural population. For South Sudan to make it; will have to have a good and ethical leader who is courageous enough to shake off tribalism and ethnic pressure, listen to the people and be determined to do well for the country.

CONCLUSION

I N 2012, THE struggle for leadership in the SPLM/A intensifies after the independence when there was a vacuum in the Nuers' military leadership. The death of Paulino Matieb and other Nuer intellectuals led to the Dinka of Bahr el Ghazal to no longer hide their intention of using the power to the maximum. The members of SPLM/A from Upper Nile, particularly Riek Machar and other intellectuals like Lam Akol and Alfred Lado which were a threat and resisted the power of the few Dinka hegemony could now be easily silenced. Kiir power could now be cemented by the power of state and the security forces. The Nuers soldiers who were brought together under General Paulino Matieb had faded significantly as the security situation in South was getting worst, only those who were organized and involve in the game of corruption would have a space to breath. It did not stop a few Nuer commanders in the army to response to the brutal killing of over 20,000 Nuer civilians in Juba. The Dinka Council of Elders and Kiir's ethnic animosities played a role in creating chaos and president Kiir's authoritarian and intolerant of criticism over corruption and bad governance as well as his secret police kept close watch on the media houses and the dissidents.

Although the competition over power is between Upper Nile and Bahr el Ghazal who are both regions controlling the military; although not to take Equatoria smile but on guard as a sleeping giant to reckon with. The Equatorians accesses to education make them to provide the personnel for the running of the government institutions, but education is not enough in the Dinka led government, the Equatorians find themselves only in the mid-managerial positions and the senior positions are led by the less educated Dinka which make them feel aggrieved and unhappy in their limited role in a state dominated by the Dinka. The Equatorians challenge has been the leadership, most of their leaders are being intimated by the Dinka leaders making them to give-in or hide behind the other groups who voice-out the graveness and had been leading to victimization of those groups.

But there is a big challenge facing the people of South Sudan under the leadership of SPLM/A, corruption wide spread all over in the country and well and alive in all the institutions including the higher level institutions such as the parliament. In 2012 South Sudan was rated the second corrupt country in the world and can also be characterized by what Mahatma Gandhi called the seven social sins. The Seven Social Sins, sometimes call the Seven Blunders of the world, is a list that Mohandas Karamchad Gandhi published in weekly newspaper Young India on October 22, 1925. (1) Later he gave this same list to his grandson, Arun Gandhi, written on a piece of paper on their final day together shortly before his assassination. (2) The Seven social Sins are:

> "Politics without principle, knowledge without character, science without humanity, wealth without work, pleasure without conscience, commerce without morality and worship without sacrifices." Rights without responsibilities were added by Arun Gandhi.

These characters can create a nation of politically incompetent population haunting by poverty, easily manipulated and led like sheep driven by fear (Watchdogs International Report 2013). I also observe the behavior of the South Sudanese increasing rudeness and I (Julia) also added my own one social sin, "pride without civility". South Sudanese have lost the pride and dignity in which they lost many of their love ones.

South Sudan faced a lot of challenges to find a system that addresses its diversity. The key idea is the creation of the constitution of their religious beliefs not only of civil society but also to the exercise of limited government authority in the sense of making laws, determining the proper application of laws, and enforcing laws. That key ideas meant that federalism (foedus), relates to the concept of covenant that really translate into human relations.

There had been heat debate on federalism among the South Sudanese with only hand full individuals, who control the power in the center rejecting federal system. The concept of covenant was applied to the constitution of society rather than being confined to purely theological discourses over forms of government.

In the realm of government, the concept was applied to village governance to counties, to states and to a limited national government associated with commonwealth. If democracies conceptualized as self-governing in the traditions of South Sudanese societies are to be viable as civilizations, they must be capable of reproducing appropriate habits of the heart and mind across succeeding generations, indefinitely to the future. The key question then is whether the society can reproduce itself and its covenantal way of life indefinitely into the future.

The viability of South Sudanese communities ways of life and its traditional autonomous con-federal arrangements for the future would depends on the development of a society of association that would enable people to give proper attentions to the crafting of institutional arrangements appropriate to a covenant societies that was and remains self-governing.

There is an anomaly, however, in western egalitarian society compare to such as in the South Sudan because the focus is on individual success while failing to recognize the fundamental vulnerability of individuals who must necessarily depend on the capabilities of others both in dealing with intergenerational cycle of life and in recognizing the cumulative cultural heritage that is necessary foundation for individual achievements (Ostrom V. 1988).

According to John Young 2012, SPLM/A did not learn from the lessons of others liberation movements such as the National Resistance Movement (NRM) in Uganda or Eritrean People's Liberation Front (EPLF) in Eritrea who defeated their enemies and ended-up developing sound institutions and economics. SPLM/A did not defeat its enemy but a got a chance to stop the war, but failed to be guided by a liberation philosophy, did not effectively mobilize the people and did not developed strong institutions to provide services to the people of South Sudan. The only thing learned by the SPLM/A is the stubbiness of Yoweri Museveni on how to manipulated the issues to control the populace and primitive militarism that left very little room for good governance and services for the people.

South Sudan could only become a country when it can reform itself with an ethical character, a need to adopt certain point of ethics character to help as criteria for selecting leaders and other constitutional post-holders. The cardinal values against leaders' behaviors or actions could be assessed on regular basis. They range from the sense of state to love of the country, civility, courtesy, moderation, respect for dignity of human life, integrity, trust, probity, primary accorded to the public interest, these are cornerstone of political and social stability. Then can we build an inclusive and cohesive society from diverse South Sudanese society that safeguards individual human rights and rule of law and a nation that will provides services such as education, health, clean water, roads to the millions of our rural communities. Putting millions our young people as the heart focus of the strategy to provide them with education that gives them dignity and honor and allows them to live their lives to the full. I believe this quote from one of the South Sudanese elder can sum it up as follow:

> 'Let us remember that we were oppressed, suffered together, fought and struggled together and now we are free together, we can therefore, be happy together in the unity and solidarity of all South Sudanese'.

But let us not forget and should be reminded by those who were before us. Rabidranath Tagore in 1910 who wrote the history during rule of 'Attila the Hun' stated that, "the scourge of the sword … throughout history it has been the violent resource of rulers who tortured and ravaged in their greed for conquest and power." South Sudan leaders are not exempted from this concept as we all have witness in our history of the liberation struggle.

I (Julia) like to recall the statement of my father Benjamin Bil Lual, a member of the Liberal Party in the 1954 Juba Conference who did not accept the federation but total separation of South Sudan. Before the debate for the fourth sitting commences he quite impatient walked up the flat form and thanked the chairman. For the proper management of the conference he politely address meeting because he was disappointed with resolution:

> "I was glad that the resolution for Federation was unanimously passed. In this I am glad and was not going to open any debate on it. But whole hearted supported the resolution. Though this was not what I expected, in fact I was expecting Separation not Federation. This is the view of my people and for this I am here in this house." (Wawa 2008)

AUTHOR NOTES

Stories of our Lives

"A well inform citizen is the strongest guardian
of his/her own liberties" Duany 2010.

WHY WE SHOULD live together? This book is largely about how our people "feel" of what had become of the movement that they labored so hard for many years. When we talked with many of our people their feelings just come out and it reminds us of Charles Dickens book, "Tale of the Two Cities." Specially, the opening line, "It was the best times, it was the worst of times, it was the epoch of incredulity". But for South Sudanese the year of 2013 was the worst of times and the dying of the dreams of liberty and prosperity.

The present situation is worse and South Sudan has been on the top of the list of fail states but Alex de Waal disputed that, 'South Sudan was never a state'. The best days are gone and when I look back so many good things were done by our leaders and sometimes we do not acknowledge them until they are gone. It is my great pleasure to share this story.

In South Sudan, when we talk about great men and women of Africa, we usually meant Nelson Mandela of South Africa, Julius Nyerere of Tanzania, Kwame Nkrumah of Ghana, Mother Teresa of moral guidance, Professor Wangari Maasi care of environment and so many others; living our own great men and women at our back yards. This is a story of understanding of one of our own great leaders from South

Sudan. This is the warmly human life story of one of the African greatest-men, one of the prime movers in South Sudanese struggle for independence and a leader whose simple, inspiring philosophy has influence many of his people and colleagues around the world.

His simple philosophy of 'Public Morality' is that, "as individual or a nation, our moral duties are not inseparable from our interest. The natural rights do guide not to commit aggression on the equal rights of others but selfishness makes a mass out of us, we become mean and greedy." Wal would always said that,

> "I feel shame when our leaders behave in way they do without understanding that, No nation, however powerful, more than individual and public opinion is the only powerful instrument of challenging a powerful nation or an individual. The man who is dishonest as state-man or woman would be a dishonest person in any situation."

This simple philosophy is an instrument of self-control and believing in self which he taught our children, tell the truth, hard work, be honest in what you do, respect and help others. His belief in building an identity is through resilience and things you identify with are what make you different from others. He installs in our children that leadership is about people and refuse to focus on your own needs.

In 2006, I was appointed the first female Undersecretary of the Ministry of Parliamentary Affairs and my office was located in the Parliament Building. Every day, I get visitors most of MPs some arguing and sometimes joking on the issues they have been debating. Those were the best days of our time, watching really nationalists concern and taking their best to find solutions to the challenges facing the country. One day I was visited by Hon. Professor Wal Duany and Hon. Dr. Toby Maduot Pareek presenting different parties, Wal, MP representing the South Sudan Democratic Forum and Maduot, MP representing Sudan

African National Union (SANU) but always vote differently in any issues, with Toby frequently supporting the ruling party SPLM.

One day Late Hon. Prof. Wal Duany and Late Hon. Dr. Toby Maduot Pareek visited my office to see me because there was a heated debate in the parliament about the issue of democratic governance and why South Sudan cannot put it together. The issues of corruption and bad governance have been challenges that the law makers were rustling with. Wal with his calm way of saying things putting his right hand on Dr. Toby's right soldered and said;

> "We cannot put ideas together my brother because we the other political parties are underdogs. The SPLM/A mechanical majority make things difficult to move in this parliament. We need ways to improve our performance in the parliament so that our people can trust us again. We have just become a rubber stamp institution with no impact to change things in our country."

Dr. Toby jumped up very angry and shaking his figure towards Wal's face and asking what he meant by calling parties dogs.

Please understand me correctly; I did not call the parties dogs. What I meant is that we are a minority who could not make any impact in this parliament. The mechanical majority is a road block to any progress in South Sudan, said Wal. Dr. Toby lowered his figure and they both sat down to continue talking on this subject. Wal asked Toby "why are you so angry? Because you know how you have been voting in this parliament, supporting a corrupt system in which you are not even benefit from all wealth SPLM/A members are controlling. All the guys in Warrap are businessmen and where are you? Just like me." Dr. Toby quickly picks it up right before Wal finishes his sentence, "even my own nephew." They both laughed so loud that their laughter invited others members of parliament into my office for a more heated debate and laughter.

What I witness, is what Hon. Prof. Wal called "a melting-pot" of South Sudan, from Raja in the west, to Akobo in the east, and from Reng in the north, to Nimule in south. From the high land of Equator, the forest of Bahr el Ghazal to the plains of Upper Nile is what Wal worked for. The small groups of people who are minorities, Makaraka, the Brun of Maban, the Jeei and Bogo are in the heart of his "Melting-pot". He always used to said, "as many hands build a house, many minds build a nation."

With current crisis in our country where we have lost over 20 thousands lives, and an estimated of 1.5 million driven from their homes while over 400,000 people have crossed into neighboring countries and over 700,000 seeking protection of UN, citizens running away from their own government is a shame on our country. I know Hon. Wal would have said something; he would have not kept quite like what most of our elders did today watching the citizens being murdered in the streets of our towns.

For those of us who kept quite we are as guilty as those who have order our young people to pick up the AK-47 to murder our incident people. We thank Hon. Prof. Peter Adwok Nyaba and Mr. Edward Lino War for being so bold in telling the truth. This is what we really need right now to save our country. As an insider in the SPLM/A he had been very bolded that South Sudan leaders have spent 10 years since CPA squandering resources and have failed to provide public goods, such as security, education, health, clean water and infrastructures and why they resorted to inciting conflict as diversionary (Nyaba 2013).

It has been a trail of tears and a heart-breaking because nothing is working in South Sudan. Every time I thought there will be a breakthrough, it never happened. I have worked on every form of development schemes in the civil society organizations, women and youth empowerment, to government in helping to formulate policies and to civil services institutional capacity-building but hardly anything worked as planned. One of the greatest excitements was when I was selected to joint our Secretary General, Mr. Abudon Agau Jok in the leadership position in our new country to draft our country Vision 2040. Our team planned everything in the country from infrastructure development, to education, health, reforms in the arm forces and all systems needed to enable the country to hit the ground running. Instead we merely hit the ground and especially with the current situation, my dreams, hopes and aspirations are dashing away.

Having the opportunity that this book affords to step back and review what has happened in South Sudan over 30 years and now, to witness the down fall of our country and missing out its fortunes, is personally moving experience and agony of a country that is bleeding. Professor Wal dream of building a nation whose democratic institutions shall have to provide robust and bring South Sudan out of it decades of war. He work all his life to addressing inequality and argued that peace is essential to human development. His flame for social justice was still strongly evidence at time he was on his hospital bed.

I would like to pay a tribute to many South Sudanese great leaders, particularly to Wal Duany; this is not a man that I call only my husband, but a mentor and a friend. I'm not only a wife but a student of Hon. Professor Wal Duany, the honest man, a Hardworking man, a Hero, who dedicated his life to labor for his nation and people. For those who will read this book, you will be joining our family in building the "melting-pot" of South Sudan through integrity, honesty, trust and respect.

Professor Wal Duany the man who earned his respect from his colleagues, locally, nationally and internationally the way he lived his life. We will miss him. May God rest his soul in peace!

HON. DR. MICHAEL WAL
DUANY EULOGY

I T IS WITH deep sorrow, great humility, and acceptance of God's will that the Duany-Wunbil family wish to inform you of the passing away of the Patriarch of our family, Honorable Dr. Michael Wal Duany, the beloved husband of Honorable Professor Julia Aker Duany, Chair of the National Recruitment Board, Ministry of Public Service, Republic of South Sudan. Dr. Wal Duany passed away on January 1, 2013 at Nairobi Hospital after a courageous and long battle with cancer.

Hon. Dr. Wal came from great family of Wunbil Urom from the Lou Nuer section of Galiek, from Buong Payam- Akobo County. Hon. Dr. Wal was born in Diror Village in 1933.

Schools attended:

He joined Wanglel Mission Elementary School in the 1948 under the former Central Nuer District- Fangak of former Upper Nile Province, presently Fangak County, Jonglei State.

Then he joined Atar Intermediate School in 1952 but at his 3rd year, he was arrested with his other colleagues of about nine in number. He was one amongst the five (5) South Sudanese taken to Swaken near Port Sudan in a hard labor prison. After 4 years hard labour, through the grace of God they were all released as a result of the Independent of the Sudan in 1956.

He joined the American Commercial High School in 1958 with John Chual Reai and late Stephen Chiec Lam in Omdurman, Sudan. He graduated in 1962. Due to lack of Nuer children access to education, their Scholarships to complete the American Commercial High School were provided by the American Mission in the Sudan and he obtained High School Diploma. Through the generosity of the American people his education development became the reality. He became one of the Nuer pioneers who hold a PH.D degree and an advocate for education, development and nation building; political tolerance and diversity in South Sudan.

Higher Education and Publications

All University education was done in United States of America (USA).

- Bachelors in Political Science from Syracuse University, New York. M. Sc in Political Science from Buffalo State University, New York. M. Sc in Public Administration from Indiana University, Indiana, USA PhD in Public Administration focuses on Constitutional Order in Political Science from Indiana University, Indiana, USA. He published "Neither Palaces Nor

Prisons: Constitutional Order Among the Nuer." He wrote extensively on Development Issues in Developing Countries.

The work experience and political Carrier.

Hon. Dr. Wal Duany worked for some time with the Christian Literature Center in Khartoum before joining the struggle in the 1960s.

He joined the Anya-nya in 1963 as the younger staff, a Secretary to Philip Pedak Lieth, the Chair of the Representative Office of the South Sudan Liberation Movement (SSLM) in Ethiopia covering the Horn of Africa. He was employed by the Radio Voice of Gospel in which he used his income to maintain the movement office in Addis Abba.

The Anya-nya movement signed the 1972 Addis Ababa Agreement and formed the first representative regional-government of the South; The High Executive Council.

Hon. Dr. Duany was passionate to bringing peace to the people of the two Sudans and lived his life with integrity, honesty, and earned the respect of his colleagues and community. He was one of the revolutionary leaders of the Anya-nya movement of South Sudan. In 1955, he was imprisoned as a teenager for resisting the oppressive regime in Khartoum for the mistreatment of the educators of the South.

Other posts held:

- Served as Representative of SSLM in North America and Israel (Anya-nya). He was the first Representative of Anya-nya to visit and seek the support of Israel, which led to strengthening the Anya-nya forces in the 1963-1972 under General Joseph Lago Yanga. Participated at the Round Table Conference 1965 and Addis Ababa Peace talks in 1972 respectively. In 1972 he became the First Minister of Cabinet Affairs, High Executive Council under the leadership of Elder Abel Alier Kwai. Served in the Parliament representing the people of Akobo County constituency on numerous occasions during the High Executive Council and as well as the National Parliament in Sudan and South Sudan Legislative Assembly (SSLA) of the Government of South Sudan 2005.

- 1983 he became Controller of the August House (High Executive Council) representing the Unity Group. Advocating United South Sudan is better off than a divided one. 1973 - Chairman of the Regional Development Corporation (RDC) he work hard to make sure that RDC become South Sudan financial independent through building local businesses. By 1976 RDC achieve its goal of financial independent with five hundred employees, over 5,000 businesses established with one Insurance Company and all Southern Industries were reconstructed, Yiol Oil Mill, Agok Fruit Company in Wau, Tony Kennaf Company, Anzera cotton farm and Textile Factory, Awiel Rice Farm, Yei Tea, Tobacco and Coffee Farm in Waatoka, others were the Cement Factory in Kapoeta, Boat Yard Factory in Juba to support fishing industry and establishment of food stores for food security all over South Sudan. 1983 - During re-division of the South, he served as Minister of Finance in Malakal, Upper Nile Region and secured 20 million developmental contracts with USAID for building infrastructure in Malakal Town. Disappointed with the leadership of D. K. Matthews on corrupt practices he resigned and was awarded scholarship to Indiana University USA. He was the Chair of the Peace and Reconciliation Conference between Jikany and Lou in Akobo, which later became known as the People-to-People Peace Process. Led New Sudan Council of Churches (NSCC) Rapporteur Team which administered the Wun-lit Peace Process. He was one of the facilitator of The Washington Conference between SPLM/A and SPLM/A-United, which produced the Washington Declaration. That document became the basis of the Comprehensive Peace Agreement under Inter Governmental Agency for Development (IGAD) in 1993.

- Co-founder of the South Sudan Friends International (SSFI), an NGO working for peace in South Sudan. Chairman and Co-founder of South Sudan Liberation Movement (SSLM) and revise the Anya-nya movement as a Commander-in-Chief of South Sudan Liberation Army (SSLA) from 2000-2005.
- Chairman and Co-founder of South Sudan Democratic Forum (SSDF) in 2001.
- Chairman of South Sudan Democratic Forum from 2012 to date.
- He participated in the making of the Interim Constitution of the Sudan as a member of National Parliament in 2005.
- In 2008 he Chair Political Parties Collisions South Sudan; he worked hard to see that democratic space should be priority in an independent new nation.

Hon Dr. Wal was a devoted Christian, faithful husband and father, trusted friend, insightful author, peace activist, intellectual, educator, and exemplary leader.

Hon. Dr. Duany is survived by his wife Prof. Julia Aker Duany; five children, sons Duany, Kueth and his wife Aprelle, and Bil; daughters Dr. Nyagon and her husband Dr. Kwadwo Amankwa, Nok and her husband Toba Bassey; and seven grandchildren, Immanuel Mal, Jinai Amaya, Sade Nyajal, Mai Bela, Bassey; Yaa Aker, and Dinai Yaw; brother, Samuel Thabac Duany, Bile Duany and sister Nyalual Duany.

The family would like to thank the people of South Sudan and all of his friends around the world for the outpouring of support in our time of grief. South Sudan has lost one his economist and developmental minded son. Our wish would be for his legacy and works to continue through those people he touched.

May he Rest in Peace.

January 04, 2013

Professor JULIA AKER DUANY

She is currently Vice Chancellor of Dr. John Garang Memorial University of Science and Technology, CEO and founder of Gender Equity and Women Leadership Program in South Sudan. Formerly Chief of Party of South Sudan Higher Education Initiative and Leadership Development, Research Associate at Vincent and Lin Ostrom Workshop in Political Theory and Policy Analysis at Indiana University. A Fulbright Scholar at Makerere University, Kampala, Uganda, She was formerly the Undersecretary in the Ministry of Parliamentary Affairs and Chairperson of Recruitment and Selection Board in the Ministry of Labour, Public Service and Human Resource Development in the Government of South Sudan (GOSS). She taught in primary and secondary schools in Sudan and United States. She and her family fled from Sudan when war broke out in 1984, and she earned her Bachelor's, Master's and Doctorate degrees from the Indiana University School of Education. Always concerned about social justice issues in her country, she co- founded the South Sudan Friends International with her husband and wrote a book entitled 'Making Peace and Nurturing Life: a Memoir of an African Woman about a Journey of Struggle and Hope'. She wrote extensively on social, justice and gender issues and she is very passionate about bringing in more South Sudanese women into political leadership roles. Winner of Dr. Martin Luther King Jr. Building Bridges Award for Faculty for dedication to service and outstanding leadership, Indiana University 2005 and Refugee Women Leadership Award for Valuable Contribution to Refugees, Women Commission for Refugees 1995, New York, USA.

ENDNOTES

AUTHOR NOTE: We are truly grateful to Late Dr. Alfred and Audrey Heasty who inspire us through their prayers and financial support. Without their support the trip could not have occurred. Thanks must also be given to the members of the Grace Covenant Presbyterian Church, Church of the Brethren, the New Sudan Council of Churches, Re. Hunter Farrell, Associate for East and West Africa, Global Mission, Lousiville, Kentucky, and the Mennonites, Late Professor Gilbert and Dorothy Weldy, the chairmen of the SPLM/A factions as well as their officers and men were all extremely cooperative and kind to us. We are thankful to all for their help and assistance.

1. In this Book when we talk of SPLM/A or SPLM/SPLA, we are referring to SPLM/A when it was <u>one </u>or before the split into two smaller liberation movements. The SPLM/A (1983-1991) included the current personnel in the SPLM/A-United. After August, 19191-1992, the new groups of the SPLM/A are referred to as "the Nasir" and "the Torit". Toward the end of 1992-1994, the SPLM/A factions identify themselves as "SPLM/A – Mainstream" under John Garang and "SPLM/A-United" under Riek Macha. We refer to them as such.

2. A wide variety of sources were used in collecting data for this report. The most important was numerous personal interviews, for a period of seven months, with both factions of SPLM/A officers, political leaders, academics, and interest groups representing women, religious organizations, and non-government organization

(NGOS). Some names of respondents are not given for the fear that if their names are known to the authorities of the movement, they can definitely get into trouble with leaders. Code names are, therefore, used. The meaning of the operational code names are as follows;

3. SPLMA/A-Mainstream /01,02, or 03; SPLM/A –United/02, 04,06 "0" stands for the official of SPLM/A-Mainstream or SPLM/A-United. "1" or "6" is a code name we gave to an official or officer of the factions for identification in our report. Names of those who were interviewed or volunteered t offer an information are not given because of their security. Such names can be released under certain conditions.

The coding of the names of those who are not officials of either of the two factions are first ci/u1, ci/u4; ci/b1 ci/b3; ci/e2, ci/e5. "ci" stands for "citizen". Citizen means a citizen of one of the regions (Upper Nile, Barh El Gharzal or Equatorial) in the South who is not a member of an executive council (which we designate as an "official") of either factions of the SPLM/A. "ul" represents two things. "U" represents Upper Nile State or Region. "1" represents the name of a citizen from the Upper Nile State that we interviewed. He/she is known in our report as ci/ul and other citizens are given different code names such as ci/u4, etc. This designation applies to citizens in other regions of Barh Ghazal and Equatoria. "b" of ci/b1 stands for Barh el Ghazal Stat. "1" is a code name of a citizen of Barh el Ghazal State. Other people who were interviewed from Barh el Gazal State and do not want their names to reveal, will be designated as ci/b3, ci/b4 etc. "e2" and "e5" represents persons from Equatoria State and follow the same pattern described in the two States of Barh el Ghazal and Upper Nile.

The second code of names of those who are not officials of the liberation movement is NGO/sl, Ngo/s4; NGO/ns3, NGO/ns5. This category distinguishes Sudanese and non-Sudanese serving in

NGOS, Thus, "s" stands for Sudanese in a given NGO. "L" OR "4" represents the individuals who have been interviewed. "n" in NGO/ns3 represents "non" Sudanese that has given us information.

4. Taban Paride, Vincen Mojowk, Joseph Gasi Abangite, Antonio Menegazzo, Gabriel Zubeir Wako, Rudolf Deng Majak, Caesar Mazeolari, Macram Max Gassis. 1992. "Letter of Sudan. Catholic Bishops to the Secretary General of the United Nations. "Khartoum: Sudan Catholic Bishop's Conference, General Secretariat. (See also Caroline Cox and John Eibner, July 14, 1993; Parliamentary Debates (HANSARD) ON Sudan. House of Lords: Official Report. Vol 541, No. 73. London: HMSO; Wal Duany 1992:2-3).

5. Joseph Lagu and many supporters of Kokora (division) substantiated this charge by showing that the Cabinet (High Executive Council) of the Regional Government in the South under Abel Alier. Dinka were more than half of the Cabinet of 18 members. He also kept his long friends of his party 'The South Front' without getting new members.

6. The meaning of the concept of covenant is further defined by Daniel Elazar, 1980: 1-30 and by Vincent Ostrom, 1991:53-68,252-253.

7. I obtained this information from an interview with Riek Machar, Chairman and Commander-in-Chief of the SPLM/A-United in November 1993 in Narobi.

The statement was also confirmed by Dr. John Garang, Chairman and Commander –in-Chief of the SPLM/A in our meeting with him in Nairobi when he talked of his support by Nuer before the split of August 1991.

8. This statement was confirmed by officials of the SPLM/A factions. We obtained the confirmation from an interview with SPLM/A-Mainstream/02 on August 29,1993 in Nairobi. I repeated this

meeting with the respondent on September 7,1993 to check the facts of the previous interview. He again confirmed the statement. We met with the respondents from SPLM/A-United 0l, 04, o8, on the 21 August, 1993 and confirmed the facts of the statement. They emphasized that the dictatorship was one of the major factors that caused rebellion against Garang.

9. This was confirmed by cl/b6 and cl/el. These individuals are active members of the southern Sudanese community in Nairobi area. They thought the article of Joseph Oduho and the paper written by Dhol Acuil Aleu were factual in contents. I interviewed cl/b6 many times in Nairobi, initial meeting was September 13,1993, and another on September, 1993 and confirmed the dissolution of the secretariat and that Garang ran the organization as his own business. The respondent was detained for years because of his critical views. Another person, the cl/el was one of the "progressive officers" of the earlier SPLM/A but he was out of the SPLM/A at the time we met. He said the leadership was ruthless and dictatorial.

10. The leadership was not prone to listen to the views of others. This is popular views among the southern Sudanese who have been in and out of the movement. Refer to footnote #9.

11. The rule of terror in the movement has been partly documented and partly we gained insights from one on one interviews. The works of Dhol Aeu, Oduho, Wantok and other former political detainees, Amnesty International report July, 1993, the U.S. Committee on Refugee's report are reasonable sources to confirm these statements. We interviewed, on numerous occasions, the SPLM/A-Mainstream/ ol, o3, o7, o11 and the SPLM/A-United/o2, o3, o5, o12. Many officials who are currently in the SPLM/A-United had contributed in the development of the political asymmetry in the movement.

12. The majority of the members of the southern Sudan Regional Assembly voted for the division of the South into smaller regions. The division was engineered by northern politicians.

13. The people who wanted the liberation of the south were convinced by the leadership of the movement that if they could force the Sudanese army out of the South, then, it would be up to the individual to proceed to the northern Sudan or stop fighting. Communist military support coming through Ethiopia was attracting officers to maintain the leadership of the liberation movement despite their dislike of communist-style instructional order.

14. The impression of the Presbyterian (USAM) peace Mission to the Sudan and to East Africa returned with an impression that there was no hope of reconciliation and unity between the SPLM/A- Factions. One member of the mission whom we referred to as NGO/ns2, told me in telephone conversation that John Garang thinks he has no contribution to the mass in the SPLM/A. "He thinks everything he does is right. "if there are no mistakes, there are no mistakes, there is no need for correction.

15. SPLM/A-Mainstream/ol told us his home in Nairobi that the Nasir Group and the Nasir Declaration has helped the South to begin to think of the liberation movement more critically. "You could not think of going to the South in those days before the Nasir Declaration," he assured us. There are positive and negative aspects of the split.

16. Cooperation between the SPLA and the southern Sudan's civil population is a key for the movement to succeed. SPLA needs support to increase the fighting force, to help in carrying ammunition, to supply food, and to help govern the South, and supply school and health services.

17. According to that report of the former political detainees, the Nuer lost their castle to the Dinka Bor, Many of their people were detained, tortured, and killed. Women and girls were raped with immunity (Wantok et al, 1992 and also footnote #29).

18. The semi-illiterates who were taken to these various communist stales for training are now officers in the fighting force in the bush. Some could become a real menace in the future. The training they had is more of indoctrination rather than learning the art of association.

19. I obtained this information from Dr. Riek Machar in an interview in Nairobi in November, 1993.

20. The less educated and uneducated were made to see the former government officials as the groups who sold out the South to the Arabs.

21. The saying of "we will liberate our country with AK-47) those who did not carry the gum are useless.

22. This process has been disrupted in the southern Sudan both by war and a lack of freedom within the free zones to exercise freedom of action and self-development.

23. Aaron Wildavsky call the culture of such groups secretariat egalitarianism (thompson, Ellis, and Wildavsky, 1990).

24. This explains is shared by both factions. Rieck Machar has attempted to harmonize the relationships between SPLA and the Western Upper Nile's civil population. But there is very little, if any, effort by the SPLM-United establish or assist villagers to reestablish civil institutions such as courts, schools and clinics.

25. For further information refer to U.S Committee for Refugees "Issue Paper" which as quantified deaths in southern Sudan. All that

deaths is not only from the Sudanese troops but also it was inflicted by SPLM/A.

26. Refer to Nasir Declaration of August 28, 1991 for further details on the principles.

27. See Nuer indigenous organization of defense system in this report.

28. The (SPLM/A-United) has been charged of violations of human rights in the attack of Bor town. Many villagers have been reported killed, SPLM/A-United has denied and maintained that Nuer who had been robbed by SPLM/A-Mainstream under Garang revenged there (see Oduho, 1992: Aleu, 1992; and Wantok el al, 1992 for more details).

29. The recent declaration of Government of Sudan has made Jonglei province into a state within the federation in the Sudan.

30. The northern Sudanese political parties which are currently members (Umma Party, DUP, Communist Party) of the NDA have ruled the South before NIF and had opportunities to work out acceptable arrangements for governance of the Sudan. Neither did that, instead fought and cause havoc in the South. NIF I one of them, it is implementing a common policy to Islamize and Arabicize the non-Moslem in the South.

31. This information was obtained in different interviews with Commander Yusif Kwo and Commander Daniel Kodi. In November, 1993 in Nairobi.

32. In Ler, Mankien, and Akobo, Upper Nile Region under the SPLM/A in September/October 1993 and Nairobi, Kenya, I was told by many persons from different ethnic groups that SPLM/A under Garang had put Nuer officers on Ethiopian helicopters to unknown destinations and dropped them from the helicopters on the way; it was reported that on one occasion, some 14 Nuer officers

were dropped from a helicopter. Thee Gaajak, Gaajok, and the Lou Nuer had suffered most in the lost of lives and property. On occasion old men, women, and children would be collected into <u>luak</u> (cattle barn), which were then set on fire. This information was obtained from a repeated interviews with more than fifty persons many of whom were officers of SPLM/A and citizens from Upper Nile, Barh el Ghazal, and Equatoria regions. (see SPLM/A-United: o1,o4,o5,o8,ci/u3,ci/u5,ci/b3,ci/b5,ci/b7,ci/b8,ci/el,ci/e3,ci/e4,ci/e6,ci/e7,ci/el1;NGO/ns3). It is also reported in Pibor and Kapoeta that persons (women, children, men of all ages) were collected into one place to be run over by tanks supplied by government of Mengistu of Ethiopia. People were not permitted to cultivate their gardens. Areas surrounding sources of drinking water have also been mined.

33. I obtained this information from an interview with John Luk Joak in Novermber, 1993 in Nairobi.

34. These meetings took place on different dates and time. Meeting with Bishop Nathaniel took place on August 25,1993 and met Mathiang Deang on August 26,1993.

35. Quoted from Robert D. Kaplan, 1993.

36. Personal interview with Pastor John Both Reath, 2016.

37. Personal interview with Gen. Tot Wei, 1996.

BIBLIOGRAPHY

Africa Information Service, ed. (1973) "Return to the Source: Selected Speeches of Amilcar Cabral." New York: Monthly Review Press.

African Union Commission of Inquiry Report on South Sudan 2014. Addis Ababa, Ethiopia.

Akol, Lam (2001) SPLA/SPLM: Inside an African Revolution (1st ed) Khartoum Press, Khartoum, Sudan.

Akol, Lam (2003) SPLM/SPLA: The Nasir Declaration. iUniverse

Akol, Lam (2007) Southern Sudan: Colonialism, Resistance and Authority. The Red Sea Press Inc. New Jersey, USA.

Aleu, Dhol Acuil (1991) "Leadership and Political Crisis in SPLM/ SPLA: A Contribution Towards Solution: Rome, Italy: Sudan People Liberation Movement/Sudan People Liberation Army.

Alier, Abel (1990) Southern Sudan: Too many Agreements Dishonored. Exerted: Ithaca Press.

Ayittey George B. N. (1991) Indigenous African Institutions. Ardsley –on-Hudson, New York: Transnational Publishers, INC.

Blandford, Neil and Jones, Bruce (1995) The World's Most Evil Men. CPI Group (UK) Ltd. Croydon, CRO 4YY.

Cabral, Amilcar (1979) <u>Unity and Struggle.</u> New York: Monthly Review Press. Collins, Robert (1971) Land Beyond Rivers: The Southern Sudan, 1990-1918. New Haven and London: Yale University Press.

Cohen, Herman J. (2015) The Mind of the African Strongman: conversations with Dictators, Statesmen and Father Figures. New Academia Publishing, Washington DC 20038-7420 USA

Dagash, Ibrahim (2006) "The OAU Reality or Fiction". OAU Information and Communication Office, UN Economic Commission for Africa, Addis Ababa

Davidons, Basil (1992) "The shadows of Neglected Ancestors". In Basil Davidson, The Black Man's Burden: Africa and the Curse of the Nation-State. New York: Time Bllik 74-98.

Davidson, Basil (1992) "The Black Man's Burden". In Basil Davidson, The Black Man's Burden: Africa and the Curse of the Nation-State. New York: Time Block 197-242.

Douglas, Mary (1980) Edward Evans-Pritchard. New York: Viking Press.

Duany, Julia A. (2003) Making Peace and Nurturing Life: A Memoir of an African Woman of Journey of Struggle and Hope. Author Books, Bloomington, Indiana, USA.

Duany, Wal (1992) "The Nuer Concept of Covenant and Covenantal Way of Life." Publius: The journal Federalism 22 (4), 67-89

Duany, Wal (1993) "The Centralization in the Sudan". Bloomington, USA: Workshop in Political Theory and policy Analysis.

Elazar, Daniel (1980) "Political Theory of Covenant "Publius: The Journal of Federalism.

Fuli, Severino (2002) Shaping a Free Southern Sudan: Memoirs of our Struggle 1934-1985. Pauline Publications, Lemur, Kenya.

Kaminski, Antoni Z. (1992) An Institutional Theory of Communist Regimes: Design, Function, and Breakdown. San Francisco: Institute for Contemporary Studies Press.

Mirghani, Ali (1986) "The Democratic Unionist Policy Towards the South." Khartoum. Newsudan Pilot Issue 20-21.

Momdani, Mahmood (2014) A speech analyzing the genesis of the South Sudan crisis, it ripple effects and the way forward, at the Annual Retreat of the National Resistance Movement at Kyankwanzi, Uganda.

National Democratic Alliance, ed. (1993) "The Nairobi Communique," Nairobi: The National Democratic Alliance (NDA).

Nyaba, Peter Aduok (2014) South Sudan: The Crisis of Infancy. Cape Town, South Africa.

Oduho, Joseph (1992) "Crisis in the Sudan People's Liberation Movement and the Sudan Peoples Liberation Army (SPLM/SPLA)," Kampala Uganda: The New Vision Newspaper.

Ostrom, Vincent (1988) "Crypto Imperialism, Predatory States, and Self-Governance. "In Vincent Ostrom, David Feeny, and Hartmut Picht, eds. Rethinking Institutional Analysis and development: Issues, Alternatives, and Choices. San Francisco: Institute for Contemporary Studies, 43-68.

Ostrom, Vincent (1993) "Comparing African and European Experiences. "Working Paper, Workshop in Political Theory and Policy analysis, Indiana University, Bloomington, Indiana, USA.

Simon, Herbert (1973) "The organization of Complex Systems. "In Hierarchy Theory; The Challenge of complex Systems, edited by Howard H. Pattee. New York, Braziller.

Soyinka, Wole (1988) "Twice Bitten: The Fate of Africa's Culture Producers "In Development and Culture, Wole Soyinka and Junzo Kawada, 1-24. New York: Africa Leadership Forum.

South Sudan: A Civil War by Any Other Name, Crisis Group Africa Report No. 217, April 10, 2014. Washington DC, USA.

The Cultural committee (1993) "On Self Determination". London: The Communist Party of the Sudan.

Young, John, (2014), The Fate of Sudan: The Origins and Consequences of a Flawed Peace Precess. Zed Book, New York, USA.

Wantok, Amon Mon, Chol Deng Alak, Edward Ater Benjamin, Deng Bior Deng, Ajiing Adiang (1992) "For a Strong SPLM/A: What is to be Done?" Nairobi, Kenya. By a Group of 1991 Former Political Detainees.

Wawa, Yosa (2008) Southern Sudanese Pursuits of Self-Determination: Documents in Political History. Marianum Press, Kisubi - Uganda